THE COUNTERHUMAN IMAGINARY

THE COUNTERHUMAN IMAGINARY

Earthquakes, Lapdogs, and Traveling Coinage in Eighteenth-Century Literature

LAURA BROWN

CORNELL UNIVERSITY PRESS
ITHACA AND LONDON

First published 2023 by Cornell University Press

Library of Congress Cataloging-in-Publication Data

Names: Brown, Laura, 1949– author.
Title: The counterhuman imaginary: earthquakes, lapdogs, and traveling coinage in eighteenth-century literature / Laura Brown.
Description: Ithaca [New York]: Cornell University Press, 2023. | Includes bibliographical references and index.
Identifiers: LCCN 2023003313 (print) | LCCN 2023003314 (ebook) | ISBN 9781501772559 (hardcover) | ISBN 9781501773242 (paperback) | ISBN 9781501772573 (pdf) | ISBN 9781501772566 (epub)
Subjects: LCSH: English literature—18th century—History and criticism. | Imagination in literature. | Human beings in literature. | Animals in literature. | Human-animal relationships in literature.
Classification: LCC PR448.I515 B76 2023 (print) | LCC PR448.I515 (ebook) | DDC 820.9/005—dc23/eng/20230406
LC record available at https://lccn.loc.gov/2023003313
LC ebook record available at https://lccn.loc.gov/2023003314

For Ka'alawai

∞

home place of our 'ohana
before we came
and after we are gone

Contents

ACKNOWLEDGMENTS

I am grateful for still-ongoing discussions with the students in my graduate seminars at Cornell University on "The Rise of the Animal," "Other Than Human Forms," "New Materialism," and "The Counterhuman Imaginary."

And I am deeply indebted to the advice, expertise, interest, support, enthusiasm, and engagement of Tita Chico, Peter Katzenstein, Felicity Nussbaum, Mahinder Kingra, and especially James Kerrigan.

A version of chapter 1 appeared in *The Eighteenth Century*, Special Issue in Honor of Felicity Nussbaum: "The Future World of Eighteenth-Century Studies," ed. Manushag Powell, 62 (2021): 153–168.

A version of chapter 2 appeared in *Robinson Crusoe after 300 Years*, ed. Andreas Mueller and Glynis Ridley (Lewisburg, PA: Bucknell University Press, 2020), 81–98.

The Counterhuman Imaginary

INTRODUCTION

The Counterhuman Imaginary

How can the human depict the other-than-human?

Works of the human imagination have recently become an explicit prov-ing ground for this disorienting question. In fact, powerful claims to depict, engage, express, affirm, and even save the other-than-human now dominate this realm of human thought. Such claims are especially visible in the theo-retical "turns" reflected in literary animal studies, new materialism, and geo-historical or ecocriticism. In literary animal studies, for example, the human attempt to acknowledge, engage, liberate, or even represent the other-than-human obviously requires human agency and its enduring implication in spe-cies hierarchy. One response to the paradox entailed in this assertion of the human power to speak for the other-than-human explicitly prioritizes liter-ature, claiming that storytelling, narrativity, or representation itself is some-how transhuman. Human storytelling is found to provide—by analogy—a subtle scenario for affirming the other-than-human, based on an imputed commonality that replaces human priority with cross-species inclusivity that transcends the human. Marion W. Copeland, in her summary of the state of the field of literary animal studies for 2012, asserts that storytelling—by definition—connects the human and the animal because "other-than-human animals have . . . language and imagination that allow them . . . to tell stories consciously based on their life experience." In her view, then, it is therefore the responsibility of human readers and authors to use literature as a way to "enter the world" of the animals "whose welfare and survival we profess," by understanding the "nonhuman, talking fictional character . . . [as] a reflection of a reality and hence a form of literary realism."[1]

This strategy is central as well to Tobias Menely's conceptualization of "voice" in *The Animal Claim*. Voice functions in Menely's argument as an analogy that—in equating the represented animal voice with the human voice and then with the political voice and then with the metaphorical voice of the assertion of rights—ultimately "continues to signify" beyond the species-specificity of the human so as to support an inclusive community of being:

> My guiding premise in this study is that human beings are always in communication with other animals, that the sociolinguistic domain . . . is only a special case in a world in which the vicissitudes of the sign provide a common condition of all living beings.
>
> . . .
>
> One of the key arguments of this book is that sensibility was concerned precisely with the way in which animal voice is remediated, translated and transformed even as it continues to signify in poetic language or in public and parliamentary debate. Sensibility offers a richly textured account of what it means to represent other animals, of how nonlinguistic injunction and address came to be refracted in the uniquely human labor of speaking for others. As a principle of advocacy, sensibility provides an important precedent for the ongoing work of animal activists and the emergence of institutions dedicated to animal protection.[2]

In a corollary way, Heather Keenleyside in *Animals and Other People* copes with the problem of human authority through an argument from literary

---

1. Marion W. Copeland, "Literary Animal Studies in 2012: Where We Are, Where We Are Going," *Anthrozoös* 25, supp. 1 (2012): s98.

2. Tobias Menely, *The Animal Claim: Sensibility and the Creaturely Voice* (Chicago: University of Chicago Press, 2015), 13, 305.

form, seeking to demonstrate that certain formal and rhetorical structures, themselves, enable human apprehension of and thus engagement with "actual" animals:

> I argue that the patently figurative animals in eighteenth-century literature have much to contribute to cultural and intellectual debates that are still with us—about the specificity of animals and the nature of species, about persons and their relationship to other sorts of creatures, and about what life is, which lives count, and how we might live together. They do this by making a point that eighteenth-century writers understood better than we: rhetorical conventions make real-world claims.[3]

Comparably, recent reflections on the representation of environmental and geological realms in literature reach into the human representation of "nature" to discover an environmentalist critique that—ethically and politically—arises from or through human creativity and at the same time seeks to extend itself toward an experience of the other-than-human realm of the environment. In *The Usufructuary Ethos: Power, Politics, and Environment in the Long Eighteenth Century*, Erin Drew tells the story of the concept of intimacy and mutuality between humans and nature—the usufructory notion of "just and legitimate uses of land and power." Drew demonstrates that in the eighteenth century this ethical and political sensibility was an influential and visible counter to Enlightenment notions of the unlimited and even inevitable human authority or dominance over the natural world.[4] In

---

3. Heather Keenleyside, *Animals and Other People: Literary Forms and Living Beings in the Long Eighteenth Century* (Philadelphia: University of Pennsylvania Press, 2017), 1. Keenelyside turns to the relevance of "actual animal lives" later in her Introduction (10). For other recent approaches to literary animals in the eighteenth century, see Lucinda Cole, *Imperfect Creatures; Vermin, Literature, and the Sciences of Life, 1600–1740* (Ann Arbor: University of Michigan Press, 2016); Ingrid Tague, *Animal Companions: Pets and Social Change in Eighteenth-Century Britain* (University Park: Pennsylvania State University Press, 2015); Laura Brown, *Homeless Dogs and Melancholy Apes: Humans and Other Animals in the Modern Literary Imagination* (Ithaca, NY: Cornell University Press, 2010); Donna Landry, *Noble Brutes: How Eastern Horses Transformed English Culture* (Baltimore: Johns Hopkins University Press, 2008); Frank Palmeri, ed., *Humans and Other Animals in Eighteenth-Century British Culture: Representation, Hybridity, Ethics* (Aldershot, UK: Ashgate, 2006); and Louse E. Robbins, *Elephant Slaves and Pampered Parrots: Exotic Animals in Eighteenth-Century Paris* (Baltimore: Johns Hopkins University Press, 2002).

4. Erin Drew, *The Usufructuary Ethos: Power, Politics, and Environment in the Long Eighteenth Century* (Charlottesville: University of Virginia Press, 2021), 4. For other recent studies of climate, ecology, and nature in the period, see Tobias Menely, *Climate and the Making of Worlds:*

exploring the literary manifestations of this counternarrative, Drew makes a strong claim for the particular—even "unique"—role of literature in "laying bare" the core human experiences of environmental transformation:

> Poetry is unique in its capacity to contain the ideological tension of simultaneously held yet incompatible beliefs, and thereby to lay bare in its full complexity the experience of living through profound cultural and material transformations while clinging to continuity. By tracing the usufructuary ethos's rise and fall through poetry, this book aims to create a better understanding not only of the environmental thought of the eighteenth century itself but of the ways a culture in the midst of environmental transformation attempts imaginatively to reckon with itself.[5]

This exercise of bringing human being into a contact of direct "reckoning" with its place in the environmental and geological realms characterizes the strong reading of literary culture offered by recent ecocriticism.

But the directness of this "reckoning" also ultimately returns to the meta-paradox generated by the presence of human agency, in this context played out as biopolitics. Leerom Medovoi offers an account of the determining status of biopolitics for the logic of ecocriticism in his essay "The Biopolitical Unconscious." Medovoi describes the "founding . . . idealistic binary of most ecocriticism, namely that between 'man' and 'nature,' 'humanity' and the 'environment,' or the 'anthropocentric' and the 'ecocentric' perspective." This binary then generates the distinguishing claim of ecocriticism, that

> if ecocriticism can inculcate an appreciation for the intrinsic value of the environment, its transformation of people's "hearts and minds" promises to liberate nature from our degradation of it. The canonization of nature writing

---

Toward a Geohistorical Poetics (Chicago: University of Chicago Press, 2021); Adeline Johns-Putra, *Climate and Literature* (Cambridge: Cambridge University Press, 2019); Tobias Menely and Jesse Oak Taylor, eds., *Anthropocene Reading: Literary History in Geologic Times* (University Park: Pennsylvania State University Press, 2017); Jeffrey Jerome Cohen and Lowell Duckert, eds., *Elemental Ecocriticism: Thinking with Air, Water, and Fire* (Minneapolis: University of Minnesota Press, 2015); Donna Landry, *The Invention of the Countryside: Hunting, Walking and Ecology in English Literature, 1672–1831* (New York: Palgrave, 2001); and James McKusick, *Green Writing: Romanticism and Ecology* (New York: St. Martin's, 2000).
    5. Drew, *Usufructuary Ethos*, 5–6.

by ecocriticism directly reflects this search for intellectual and artistic traditions within which this intrinsic value of nature is recognized and honored. . . . [But] the history of biopolitics teaches us that ecocriticism's binary opposition of man and environment (aligned with bad anthropocentric and good biocentric thinking respectively) is utterly ahistorical. . . . This system of biopolitics remains a human creation.[6]

Access to the experience of the other-than-human through literary critique, for Medovoi, then, must instead involve a study of *"the mode of production at the level of its biopolitical self-regulation"* and of the text as "the ideology of literary form itself in its unconscious relationship to transitions between modes of production."[7] Medovoi's position acknowledges and incorporates conceptually the fundamental paradox inherent in claims for the direct apprehension, reckoning, or advocacy of the other-than-human through the human imagination. His methodology, as we shall see, is corollary to the theorizations of "cosmological criticism" or "geohistorical contradiction" proposed by Edna Duffy in her "cosmological" account of Fredric Jameson's *Political Unconscious* and by Tobias Menely in his *Climate and the Making of Worlds*—both of which we will engage in a summary concession to the unimaginable "just beyond" of the counterhuman imaginary, in the coda to this study.[8]

New materialist theory also encounters this pervasive meta-paradox of the asserted contact between the human and the other-than-human—in this context, the terms of the paradox are generated by an assumed connection between the idea of the intrinsic vitality of matter per se and the activity of the human imagination in its representation of that vitality and of the material world. And again, in the new materialist context, the account of this leveling alignment of the human with the material thing is presented as a distinctive or even unique feature of literature—inherent in the activity of the human imagination. This symptomatic and tempting claim—that human

---

6. Leerom Medovoi, "The Biopolitical Unconscious: Toward an Eco-Marxist Literary Theory," in *Literary Materialisms*, ed. Mathias Nilges and Emilio Sauri (New York: Palgrave Macmillan, 2013), 85–86.

7. Medovoi, 87.

8. Menely, *Climate and the Making of Worlds*; Edna Duffy, "Modernism under Review: Fredric Jameson's *The Political Unconscious: Narrative as a Socially Symbolic Act* (1981)," *Modernist Cultures* 11 (2016): 143–160.

creativity through its own vitality offers special access to the vitality of matter—is expressed from a range of perspectives. Jane Bennett in *Vibrant Matter* uses the approach to literature as the explicit methodological model for the engagement with the vibrant nature of matter, suggesting that literature entails or inculcates a special "attentiveness" to things:

> What method could possibly be appropriate for the task of speaking a word for vibrant matter? How to describe without thereby erasing the independence of things? How to acknowledge the obscure but ubiquitous intensity of impersonal affect? . . . What is . . . needed is a cultivated, patient, sensory attentiveness to nonhuman forces operating outside and inside the human body. I have tried to learn how to induce an attentiveness to things . . . from Thoreau, Franz Kafka, and Whitman.[9]

The same tactic is implied in Richard Grusin's *The Nonhuman Turn*; the opening assertion of this volume's introduction describes the originary value of the canonical works of the American literary tradition in modeling the special attention to the other-than-human that we are now called on to acknowledge. In Grusin's words, "in American literature . . . we can trace this concern [with nonhumans] back at least to Emerson, Thoreau, Melville, Dickinson, and Whitman."[10]

Suggestions as to how this unique literary access to the other-than-human might be defined or exercised are symptomatically complex for new materialist critique. Rick Dolphijn and Iris van der Tuin in their introduction to *New Materialism: Interviews and Cartographies* describe a kind of "entanglement" of matter and meaning distinctive to the experience of art:

> New materialism allows for the study of the [material and discursive dimensions of art] in their entanglement: the experience of a piece of art is made up of matter *and* meaning. The material dimension creates *and* gives form to the discursive, and vice versa. Similar to what happens with the artwork, new materialism sets itself to rewriting events that are usually only of interest to natural scientists. Here it becomes apparent that a new materialist take on

---

9. Jane Bennett, *Vibrant Matter: A Political Ecology of Things* (Durham, NC: Duke University Press, 2010), xiii–ix.

10. Richard Grusin, introduction to *The Nonhuman Turn*, ed. Grusin (Minneapolis: University of Minnesota Press, 2015), viii.

"nature" will be shown to be transposable to the study of "culture" and vice versa, notwithstanding the fact that these transpositions are not unilinear.[11]

And for Diana Coole and Samantha Frost, in the introductory overview of the field for their volume *New Materialisms: Ontology, Agency, and Politics*, the capacity for symbolism—which, they argue, has been too narrowly attributed to the human—transcends species and participates in a "spectrum" whose scope itself entails generativity and vitality:

> The new materialism does prompt a way of reconsidering [capacities for symbolism or reflexivity] as diffuse, chance products of a self-generative nature from which they never entirely emerge. It further invites acknowledgment that these capacities are manifest in varying degrees across different species of being, that they are indelibly material in their provenance, that human intelligence emerges within a spectrum of vital materializations.[12]

Symbolism serves for Coole and Frost the same conceptual purpose that we have seen human/animal storytelling serve for Copeland or voice for Menely: offering an imputed commonality as the basis for the claim for human access to the other-than-human. But Coole and Frost seek to complicate the conceptualization of that access through their use of the notion of "spectrum"—a direct corollary to Dolphijn and van der Tuin's "entanglement"—both of which evoke an ongoing elusive interrelationality and which indicate the challenge of describing coherently, much less defining, the actual product of human creativity as it claims to access the realm of matter.

But, fundamentally, any asserted human access to the other-than-human is confounded by the indisputable intervention of the human in that process. The notion of the "counterhuman imaginary" proposed in this book respects this paradox by incorporating it conceptually—by situating the problem of the human representation of the other-than-human within the concept of the "cultural imaginary" as a way of intentionally unsettling human authority

---

11. Rick Dolphijn and Iris van der Tuin, "Introduction: A 'New Tradition' in Thought," in *New Materialism: Interviews and Cartographies*, ed. Dolphijn and van der Tuin (Ann Arbor: UM Publishing, University of Michigan Library, Open Humanities Press, 2012), 91.

12. Diana Coole and Samantha Frost, "Introducing the New Materialisms," in *New Materialisms: Ontology, Agency, and Politics*, ed. Coole and Frost (Durham, NC: Duke University Press, 2010), 21.

or veracity in advance of any explication or any experience of the other-than-human within human discourse. The first step must be an acknowledgment of human-centered assumptions. In thus systematically circumscribing human access to authenticity or authority regarding the realms beyond those of human being, the concept of the "counterhuman imaginary" in this study calls on the theory of the "cultural imaginary" as expressed in the historical materialist framework developed by Louis Althusser and Cornelius Castoriadis.

The Althusserian notion of ideology offers an account of the human subject that systematically repudiates straightforward or direct contact between the human and the realms beyond the human—social, political, or natural. Though the human subject might assume for itself a relationship with those realms, that relationship, Althusser argues, is fundamentally shaped by the processes of "ideological interpellation" by which the human subject is called by and reflects, absorbs, and embraces the ever-present social and political and institutional structures within which they are embedded.[13] Post-Marxist studies of ideology have variously sought to move from Althusser's focus on social and political doctrines or systems to an attention to cultural, institutional, psychic, and discursive structures. John B. Thompson in *Studies in the Theory of Ideology* describes the scope of these contributions that move Althusserian theory toward the cultural and psychic. He begins with an appraisal of the important contribution of Cornelius Castoriadis to "the key question of the imaginary," which "is to be conceived . . . as the *creative core* of the social-historical and psychic worlds, . . . the element which creates *ex nihilo* the figures and forms that render 'this world' and 'what is' possible."[14] Castoriadis in his *Imaginary Institution of Society* sees the cultural imaginary as a creation that

> overdetermines the choice and the connections of symbolic networks, which is the creation of each historical period, its singular manner of living, of seeing and of conducting its own existence, its world, and its relations with this world. . . .
>
> [This] originary structuring component, this central signifying-signified, the source of that which presents itself in every instance as an indisputable

13. Louis Althusser, *On the Reproduction of Capitalism: Ideology and Ideological State Apparatuses* (1969), trans. G. M. Goshgarian (London: Verso, 2013).

14. John B. Thompson, *Studies in the Theory of Ideology* (Berkeley: University of California Press, 1984), 36.

and undisputed meaning, the basis for articulating what does matter and what does not, the origin of the surplus of being of the objects of practical, affective and intellectual investment, whether individual or collective—is nothing other than the *imaginary* of the society.[15]

That "central signifying-signified"—the precondition of any human representation—is immediately relevant to the meta-paradox entailed in the human claim to access to the other-than-human. The notion of the cultural imaginary systematically proscribes ultimate or unconditional human authority and frames any human account of "'this world' and 'what is' possible" as "nothing other than the *imaginary* of the society."[16]

The "counterhuman imaginary" of this study directly acknowledges the "imaginary" nature of claims of human representation and human authority, in order to discover the "counterhuman" disruptions that are generated out of or alongside those claims through the self-efficacy of the other-than-human. That self-efficacy is the subject of the following chapters, to the extent that it can be interpolated alongside or in a contrapuntal relation to the human cultural imaginary. In other words, the conceptual scenario of *The Counterhuman Imaginary* works on the axis of the meta-paradox of human access to the other-than-human, to project along that axis an other-than-human experience, reflective of an other-than-human vitality or agency or force. By framing the explication of the other-than-human in relation to the cultural imaginary, the concept of the "counterhuman" comes back to the text itself, acknowledging the implication in and the relevance of the other-than-human in the imaginative products of the human imagination. In this sense, the critique demonstrated here focuses on an enrichment of our understanding—and even appreciation—of the ultimate scope and even power of the literary.

I

As a disruptive or counterintuitive experience, the counterhuman presents a persistent challenge and opportunity for explication and for methodological

---

15. Cornelius Castoriadis, *The Imaginary Institution of Society*, trans. Karen Blamey (Cambridge, MA: MIT Press, 1987), 145 (originally published as *L'institution imaginaire de la société*, 1975).
16. Thompson, *Studies in the Theory of Ideology*, 36.

innovation—a challenge that is endemic to its premise and that is also, symptomatically, relevant to current approaches that question the authority or naturalness or individuality of the human. A significant and fertile corollary to the methodology of the counterhuman imaginary is to be found in the "affective turn."[17] A key dimension of affect theory pursues a perspective that intersects directly with the counterhuman through the experience of inter-relationality. "In-between-ness" or "occurent relation," to use Brian Massumi's working terms, offers a methodological avenue along which the counterhuman might intersect with the *transindividual*.[18] In Massumi's words,

> If there is one key term [in the definition of affect], that's it: relation. When you start in-between, what you're in the middle of is a region of relation. . . .

> But it is even more important to realize that "pre-subjective" in this usage means *transindividual*. . . . First, in the sense . . . that it pertains directly to what is passing *between* the individuals involved, which is reducible to neither taken separately. And second, in the sense that it coincides with a *becoming* of the involved individuals.[19]

Following Massumi, Stephen Ahern in "Affect Theory Reads the Age of Sensibility" directly raises the issue of species difference. Ahern argues in his explication of "moments of affective agitation [in] the face-to-face encounter with alterity . . . that affect is autonomous (even 'pre-personal')" and characterized "by the modulations of a 'field of forces.'" And he suggests that "such modulations can be analyzed in a dynamic system that includes affectual relations among human, animal, and even inorganic actants." Ahern thus claims that affect theory promises

> a breaking through of the categories of difference that keep us apart—an effacing of socioeconomic, generational, gendered, racial, even species difference.

---

17. Aleksondra Hultquist in her overview account of the "affective turn" usefully differentiates between the "history of emotion" and "affect theory": "Scholars asking history of emotion questions are interested in the cultural, psychological, and historical contingencies of how we feel what we feel"; while for affect theorists, affects are "prepersonal," "precognitive," "highlighting difference, process, and force" (citing Brian Massumi, Melissa Gregg and Gregory J. Seigworth, and Margaret Wetherall). Hultquist, "Introductory Essay: Emotion, Affect, and the Eighteenth Century," *The Eighteenth Century* 58 (2017): 274.

18. Brian Massumi, *Politics of Affect* (Cambridge, UK: Polity, 2015), 94.

19. Massumi, 50, 94.

It's as if in moments of suspension, when bodies are impinging on one another, affecting and affected, but between states, in an *in-between-ness* that affect theorists have sought to highlight, in a *not-yet* state of potential for change, there is a space for neutrality in which power imbalances might be cancelled out, and affective assemblages created that offer newly born communities primed to act, resistant to dualistic thinking, of the reign of me versus you, of us versus them.[20]

We will see a performance of this *in-between-ness* from the perspective of the counterhuman imaginary in the analysis of "species intimacies" in chapter 1. There, as we see in the lapdog lyric and the circulation narrative, the suffusion of the human into the other-than-human and the destabilization of human affectivity through transspecies melding use radical interrelationality to step beyond conventional or hierarchical boundaries and to project an experience of ontological uncertainty—even of an innovative "community"—indigenous to the counterhuman.

The concept of the disruptive impact of the counterhuman finds another corollary methodology in revisionist approaches to the definition of the human itself. Lynn Festa's rich and detailed account of the function of the other-than-human in eighteenth-century literature, *Fiction without Humanity*, argues that "person and thing, human and animal, are intertwined rather than opposed": "Rather than starting from a presumptive (human) subject and adding predicates or appealing to preestablished binaries of person and thing, human and animal, I show how writers use anthropomorphized animals and personified things to investigate humanity's own creaturely and thinglike nature."[21] The consequence for Festa's

---

20. Stephen Ahern, "Nothing More Than Feelings? Affect Theory Reads the Age of Sensibility," *The Eighteenth Century* 58 (2017): 286, 287–88. For other relevant studies and statements on affect theory, see Sara Ahmed, *Cultural Politics of Emotion* (New York: Routledge, 2014); Ruth Leys, "The Turn to Affect," *Critical Inquiry* 37 (2011): 434–72; William E. Connolly, *A World of Becoming* (Durham, NC: Duke University Press, 2011); Melissa Gregg and Gregory J. Seigworth, eds., *The Affect Theory Reader* (Durham, NC: Duke University Press, 2010); Melissa Gregg and Gregory J. Seigworth, "An Inventory of Shimmers," in Gregg and Seigworth, *Affect Theory Reader*, 1–25; Patricia Ticineto Clough and Jean Halley, eds., *The Affective Turn: Theorizing the Social* (Durham, NC: Duke University Press, 2007); and Eve Kosofsky Sedgwick, *Touching Feeling: Affect, Pedagogy, Performativity* (Durham, NC: Duke University Press, 2003).

21. Lynn Festa, *Fiction without Humanity: Person, Animal, Thing in Early Enlightenment Literature and Culture* (Philadelphia: University of Pennsylvania Press, 2019), 1, 2. Subsequent references to this source are cited parenthetically in the text. For recent studies relevant to objects and

analysis is that literature enables readers "to adopt [the] radically new and alien perspectives" (35) of objects, instruments, or animals. By doing so, literature "produces"—or "elicits," "interpellates," "projects," "performs," or "constitutes"—the human, by using "anthropomorphized animals and personified things to investigate humanity's own creaturely and thinglike nature" (60, 8, 9, 15, 2). The "radical" or "alien" dissonance between the interpellated human and other-than-human "forces" here is our common conceptual problematic (4). Both for Festa's argument and for the concept of the counterhuman imaginary, that dissonance provides an ongoing methodological challenge and opportunity. Like Festa's "processual" model (31), the counterhuman imaginary also positions—or destabilizes— the human as the product of a process of interpellation. And the counter- human imaginary—also like Festa's process—locates the other-than- human in disruptive proximity to human assertions of authority. But in this study, the *counterhuman* systematically foregrounds and explicates the "radically new and alien" form of that dissonance, in order to generate a methodology that makes the experience of the other-than-human percep- tible on an axis *counter* to, rather than—as for Festa—constitutive of or absorbed by, the human.

And this experience of perceptibility also has an illuminating point of con- tact with Bill Brown's definition of "things-in-themselves" in "Things—in Theory," the opening chapter of *Other Things*. In this essay, Brown offers a "clarification"—in the form of a kind of reverse provocation: "My concern is not with whether you succeed or fail to grasp things-in-themselves, objects as they are. My concern is how objects grasp you."[22] *How objects grasp you* is a subject-oriented expression of the meta-paradox at hand for *The Counter- human Imaginary*. Working through Heidegger, DeLillo, and Lacan, Brown

---

"things" in eighteenth-century studies, see Helen Thompson, *Fictional Matter: Empiricism, Cor- puscles, and the Novel* (Philadelphia: University of Pennsylvania Press, 2017); Sean Silver, *The Mind Is a Collection: Case Studies in Eighteenth-Century Thought* (Philadelphia: University of Pennsylva- nia Press, 2015); Jonathan Lamb, *The Things Things Say* (Princeton, NJ: Princeton University Press, 2011); Jonathan Kramnick, *Actions and Objects from Richardson to Hobbes* (Stanford, CA: Stanford University Press, 2010); Julie Park, *The Self and It: Novel Objects and Material Subjects in Eighteenth- Century England* (Stanford, CA: Stanford University Press, 2009); Mark Blackwell, ed., *The Secret Lives of Things: Animals, Objects, and It-Narratives in Eighteenth-Century England* (Lewisburg, PA: Bucknell University Press, 2007); and Cynthia Wall, *The Prose of Things: Transformations of De- scription in the Eighteenth Century* (Chicago: University of Chicago Press, 2006).

22. Bill Brown, *Other Things* (Chicago: University of Chicago Press, 2015), 23.

here describes the meta-paradox of the thing variously and eloquently. It is "immediate," "self-contained," and "independent"; it demonstrates a "stubborn evasion . . . from our thought," a "self-refusal," and an "unconditioned autonomy" that reflects "the abyss of the real." It "discloses itself" only through "accident, confusion, emergency, contingency," and then only through the work of art.[23] As we shall see, the concept of the counterhuman specifies this autonomy and this abyss by enabling the self-efficacious forces of the other-than-human to disclose themselves through the counterhuman dimensions of literary creativity.

This disclosure—the "radical and alien" impact of *how objects grasp you*—is aligned with the recent engagement with "postcritique": the turn from the skeptical, diagnostic, symptomatic, suspicious, or oppositional modes of analysis that have characterized modern literary critique. In the introduction to *Critique and Postcritique*, Elizabeth S. Anker and Rita Felski provide an overview and evaluation of "critique as a genre":

> While the association of critique with self-questioning extends back to Kant, it is heightened and intensified in the "dramas of exposure" that characterize contemporary forms of interpretation. Whatever is natural, taken for granted, essentialized, or transparent becomes the critic's target: such qualities are seen as not only theoretically inadequate (in failing to acknowledge the linguistic and cultural construction of reality), but also politically troubling (in "naturalizing" social phenomena and thereby rendering them immune to criticism and change). As a result, critique has encouraged a recurring preoccupation with second-order or meta-analysis and a seemingly inexhaustible relay of skepticism and disclosure: hermeneutic insight emerges only to become the object of further suspicion, lest it fall prey to the stable, authentic, or authoritative knowledge that critique seeks to challenge. Demanding a hyper-vigilance on the part of the critic, critique thus requires stringent self-critique and continued attempts to second-guess or "problematize" one's own assumptions.[24]

23. Brown, 39, 18, 28, 39, and 32. In these contexts, Brown variously cites Heidegger from *What Is a Thing?* and "The Origin of the Work of Art." See Martin Heidegger, *What Is a Thing?*, trans. W. B. Barton Jr. and Vera Deutsch (Chicago: Henry Regnery, 1967), 7; and Heidegger, "The Origin of the Work of Art," in *Poetry, Language, Thought*, trans. Albert Hofstadter (New York: Perennial, 2001), 31, 67.

24. Elizabeth S. Anker and Rita Felski, introduction to *Critique and Postcritique*, ed. Anker and Felski (Durham, NC: Duke University Press, 2017), 3, 8.

The broad effort of postcritique is to highlight an immediate engagement with the text—this engagement involves, for Felski and Anker, "treating texts with respect, care, and attention, emphasizing the visible rather than the concealed in a spirit of dialogue and constructiveness rather than dissection and diagnosis. . . . What gets built and shaped when a critic reads? What affordances and opportunities does literary form and experience open up?"[25] Recent claims for "surface reading," "thin description," or "reparative reading" foreground the affirmation, embodiment, and autonomy that emerge from that experience and that attention.[26] Jonathan Culler, for example, describes the "capacious appreciation" of the text that results from his approach to poetry in his *Theory of the Lyric*: "our attention should be directed to experiencing the poem itself as an event."[27]

The concept of the counterhuman imaginary steers literary interpretation between critique and postcritique, by moving through the constructivist hermeneutic insight of the Althusserian or Castoriadian *imaginary* to a first-order experience of the impact of the other-than-human on and through the literary text—in an immediate *grasp* of the self-efficacy of matter, a sustained implication in intra-activity, a "radical" overwriting of species boundaries and of affects, or a self-efficacious manifestation of pervasive, horizontal, unwitnessed turbulence. An account and an "appreciation" of how a poem might *grasp* the reader *as an event* locates counterhuman interpretation within rather than beyond the text.

The idea of the counterhuman also points toward the posthuman—a current concept with a wide scope, which Rosi Braidotti in *The Posthuman* has described as the "explosion" or the "qualitative shift in our thinking about . . . the basic unit of common reference for our species, our polity and our relationship to the other inhabitants of this planet."[28] Posthumanism—or, vari-

---

25. Anker and Felski, 16, 20.

26. Anker and Felski cite, as now-classic examples, Stephen Best and Sharon Marcus, "Surface Reading: An Introduction," *Representations* 108 (2009): 1–21; Sedgwick, *Touching Feeling*; and Heather Love, "Close but Not Deep: Literary Ethics and the Descriptive Turn," *New Literary History* 41 (2010): 371–91.

27. Jonathan Culler, *Theory of the Lyric* (Cambridge, MA: Harvard University Press, 2015), 349–50.

28. Rosi Braidotti, *The Posthuman* (Cambridge, UK: Polity, 2013), 1–2. Recent explications of the "posthuman" include theoretical, ontological, and cultural scenarios. On ontology, see Donna Haraway, *The Companion Species Manifesto: Dogs, People, and Significant Otherness* (Chicago: Prickly Paradigm, 2003). On the literary representation of sympathy for or identification with ani-

ously, transhumanism, hyperhumanism, antihumanism, or metahumanism—
has developed across the arenas of critical and cultural theory, anthropology,
molecular biology, technology, neuroscience, environmental studies, and
quantum physics.[29] Braidotti offers a summary account of "the common denominator for the posthuman": "an assumption about the vital, self-organizing
and yet non-naturalistic structure of living matter itself . . . supported by a
monistic philosophy, which rejects dualism, especially the opposition nature-
culture, and stresses instead the self-organizing (or auto-poietic) force of living
matter."[30] Francesca Ferrando's systematic account of the scope of the perspective of the posthuman further engages anthropocentrism and speciesism:

> Posthumanism is often defined as a post-humanism and a post-anthropocen-
> trism: it is "post" to the concept of the human and to the historical occur-
> rence of humanism, both based . . . on hierarchical social constructs and
> human-centric assumptions. Speciesism has turned into an integral aspect of
> the posthuman critical approach. The posthuman overcoming of human
> primacy, though, is not to be replaced with other types of primacies. . . .
> Posthumanism is a post-centralizing, in the sense that it recognizes not one
> but many specific centers of interest; it dismisses the centrality of the centre
> in its singular form, both in its hegemonic as in its resistant modes. . . . Its
> perspectives have to be pluralistic, multilayered, and as comprehensive and
> inclusive as possible. . . . Posthumanism does not stand on a hierarchical
> system: there are no higher and lower degrees of alterity, when formulating

---

mals, see John Morillo, *The Rise of Animals and Descent of Man, 1660–1800: Toward Posthumanism
in British Literature between Descartes and Darwin* (Newark: University of Delaware Press, 2018).
For perspectives highlighting deconstruction, see Stefan Herbrechter's account of "critical posthumanism . . . as a continuation of . . . [the] deconstruction of the subject," in *Posthumanism: A
Critical Analysis* (London: Bloomsbury, 2013), 197; originally *Posthumanismus: Eine knitishe Ein-
fuhrung* (2009). And see Cary Wolfe's focus on posthumanism as a response to the "deeply problematic" construction of the humanist subject *"especially"* within 'linguacentric' disciplines such as
cultural criticism . . . [making] even the possibility of subjectivity coterminous with the species
barrier," in "The Second-Order Cybernetics of Maturana and Varela," *Cultural Critique* 30 (1995):
35; and also Wolfe, *What Is Posthumanism?* (Minneapolis: University of Minnesota Press, 2010.

29. For a conceptual account of the current terms and concepts relevant to "posthumanism,"
see Francesca Ferrando, "Posthumanism, Transhumanism, Antihumanism, Metahumanism, and
New Materialisms: Differences and Relations," *Existenz* 8 (2013): 26–32. I am indebted to Peter J.
Katzenstein's account of the posthuman and especially the transhuman, notably in his recent
"Worldviews and World Politics," in *Uncertainty and Its Discontents: Worldviews in World Politics*,
ed. Katzenstein (Cambridge: Cambridge University Press, 2022), 1–69.

30. Braidotti, *Posthuman*, 2–3.

a posthuman standpoint, so that the non-human differences are as compelling as the human ones. Posthumanism is a philosophy which provides a suitable way of departure to think in relational and multi-layered ways, expanding the focus to the non-human realm in post-dualistic, post-hierarchical modes, thus allowing one to envision post-human futures which will radically stretch the boundaries of human imagination.[31]

This "radical" "stretching"—toward what might even be termed an inexpressible realm *beyond* the human—first requires, for a human approach to posthumanism, a foothold in the *counterhuman*: the counterhuman imaginary supplies a formal locus for the experience of the posthuman. The aspects of the counterhuman that become visible through an explication of the contrapuntal effects that accrue to the presumed authority of the human cultural imaginary offer a means of approaching that "radical" space "beyond the boundaries of human imagination"—a glimpse of the "self-organizing force" of the other-than-human that is otherwise inaccessible to the human.

In animal studies, new materialist theory, and environmental or geohistorical criticism, the notion of the "actuality" of animals, the "independence" of things, or the immediacy of the human "reckoning" with nature all project—as the ultimate scene of analysis—a lifeworld to which, as we have seen, literature is asserted to have a special access. That claim to access often unproblematically assumes—even asserts—the efficacy, the power, and the authority of the human. But if we take on the literary experience of the other-than-human from the perspective of the human cultural imaginary, and if we focus then on relations within that imaginary scenario rather than on some purported reality beyond it, and if, within that realm, we provide an account of the self-efficacy of the other-than-human as a contrapuntal engagement that operates against or beyond or tangentially through human representation, then animals, things, or environmental and geological factors can be seen to exert a distinctive force—a "self-organizing" efficacy— even within the "indisputable and undisputed" meaning-making by which human being imagines its own existence. The premise of this study, then, is that animals, things, and environmental and geological elements and events are always generating counterhuman pressures on human discourse—they are always generating a counterhuman imaginary. A systematic attention to those

---

31. Ferrando, "Posthumanism," 29.

counterhuman pressures offers insights that look across the broad range of "posthuman" perspectives that have variously sought to engage the other-than-human: affect theory, new materialism, animal studies, and ecocriticism.

This study tests the analytical opportunities provided by the notion of the counterhuman imaginary by focusing on a diverse set of influential literary texts from the early eighteenth century in England. These pressures of the other-than-human within the human imagination belong to the whole history of human creativity. But the particular historical context of this book illuminates the status of the counterhuman imaginary at a significant moment in the history of humans, animals, and the geographical and environmental realm—a moment that involves what is often understood as the constitution of human modernity. As I have argued elsewhere, the transformations in economic, social, cultural, and intellectual history that mark this moment—the rapid and substantial developments in production, profit, and trade; in exploration, expansion, and imperialism; in urbanization, bureaucracy, and the extension of private property; and in approaches to metaphysics, ontology, and to the understanding of the material world—are all variously and powerfully felt in and through the literary imagination in the eighteenth century.[32]

The texts studied here reflect a sample of scenarios from across these transformations and thus offer a set of particular opportunities to discover and define the impact of the counterhuman on distinctive occasions in the human engagement with the cultural imaginary—with the representation of "'this world' and 'what is' possible" in the English eighteenth century. The transformative shift in the metaphysical and empirical conceptualization of the hierarchy of being—the replacement of the "chain" with new principles of continuity and plenitude—creates an opportunity for the generic innovation produced by the counterhuman melding of beings analyzed in chapter 1. The Newtonian reshaping of "the entire conception of matter" provides an immediately pertinent condition for the analysis of counterhuman force in chapter 2 as well as in chapter 3.[33] Meanwhile trade, circulation, and the proliferative presence of the marketplace shape the urban context of *The*

---

32. Laura Brown, *Fables of Modernity: Literature and Culture in the English Eighteenth Century* (Ithaca, NY: Cornell University Press, 2001), 4–11.

33. Ernan McMullin, *Newton on Matter and Energy* (Notre Dame, IN: University of Notre Dame Press, 1979), 1.

Dunciad in chapter 3 and the global scenario of the circulating banknote in chapter 1. Chapter 4 on the Lisbon earthquake tests the relevance of the counterhuman to a singular, specific, global geologic event—the transformation of the Earth itself on the date of November 1, 1755, human time—and explores the intersections of that event with Enlightenment discourse and debate. And the rise in the urgency, distribution, and asserted authority of modern reporting and journalism is a core context for chapter 5 on the Great Storm of 1703. Exposing the operations of the disruptive forces of the other-than-human within the human cultural imaginary at this particular and transitional juncture in the history of human creativity—the English eighteenth century—calls attention to both the specificity and the breadth of the counterhuman. And meanwhile, the distinctive scenarios considered here may also offer, in turn, models for other, ongoing accounts of the vitality and self-efficacy of the other-than-human across the larger-than-human history.

II

The chapters that follow focus on five distinct instances of the literary enactment of the counterhuman imaginary that engage these historical transformations, building through the explication of each text or literary form a critical method that attends to the dynamic of the other-than-human, within and beyond the human cultural imaginary. These chapters track the scope of the emergence of the other-than-human across prose fiction and journalistic narrative, lyric and narrative poetry, and canonical works and popular subgenres, to emphasize the pervasiveness of the other-than-human in the literary culture of this period, which is conventionally and famously associated with the "rise of the novel" and the primacy of the human, individualist protagonist. And these distinct explications of the counterhuman also track the range of its demeanors in relation to the literary imagination. In these texts, the "radical" "stretching" of the boundaries of the human imagination entailed by the counterhuman takes corollary forms, which align with the intrinsic force, the self-efficacy, and the uncentered interrelationality of the posthuman. The uncentered relationality of the counterhuman can generate a systematic ontological uncertainty that unseats the centrality of human affect and "love" by representing intimacies across forms of being and of matter, thus usurping the affective properties of the human. The counterhuman can indicate the energy of the material other-than-human thing to move "on its own"—its "inexpressible" force and its intrinsic capacity to populate the world through a proliferative sequence of accumulation. It can pointedly replace human being with moving matter that operates through an ongoing "intra-action" or fluctuation or flattening and that intimates—more broadly—an ultimate "chaos" or "abyss" or even the "uncreation" or the transcendence of the human. And the counterhuman can be projected beyond human authority, as an unaccountable multiplicity, an inexplicable and immediate force, or as an impossible confluence irrelevant to human agency—a "tumbling," cascading, unlimited, and undirected flood.

Movement beyond the bounds of human convention is a key scenario for the counterhuman imaginary across a range of literary contexts. Chapter 1, "Species Intimacies: Lapdogs and Banknotes," argues that two popular eighteenth-century subgenres—one depicting lapdogs and the other generating protagonists from banknotes, sedan chairs, and overcoats—create corollary counterhuman experiments in multiplicity and immeasurability. This chapter juxtaposes the lapdog lyric and the circulation narrative in order to explore imaginative scenarios that focus on affective substitution and "love." Both the lapdog lyric and the circulation narrative place human being into surprising, direct, intimate contact with the other-than-human. The circulation narrative uses that contact to represent the affective merging of the human with the material thing in the form of a thing-protagonist; that thing-protagonist exhibits a suffusion with human emotion in a way that ultimately makes the thing into a human equivalent. In the case of the lapdog lyric, the poetry celebrating the "love" between the lady and the lapdog consistently represents a corporeal cross-species intimacy that challenges human-centered conventions of affinity. Both of these subgenres reach toward a counterhuman imagining of affect based on an unconventional or immeasurable experience of cross-species movement.

"Active Matter, Vital Force: The Mobilization of Matter: Newton and Defoe," Chapter 2, lays out the discursive underpinnings of other-than-human force for the modern imagination through a comparison of Newton's *Optics* and Defoe's *Robinson Crusoe*. In the language of the *Optics*, the focus on "experienced bodies" asserts the capacity of matter to attract or pull or "act," an agency that is itself enacted in Newton's gravitational theory. In Defoe's narrative, also, things act by populating the "desert" island through the ongoing activity of irresistible succession: the autonomous generation of things from things. This chapter argues that these corollary discourses of autonomy and of irresistible succession create a form of counterhuman motion, in which matter moves beyond or without or separately from the human. Both Newton's and Defoe's texts show matter moving and demonstrate a counterhuman imaginative impact irrelevant to the conventional critical focus on the agency of the novelistic human protagonist.

Irresistible motion connects the counterhuman impact of the *Optics* and *Robinson Crusoe* with Alexander Pope's mock-heroic poem *The Dunciad*. Chapter 3, "The Uncreation of the Human: Pope's *Dunciad*," takes up the "force inertly strong" that flows through *The Dunciad*'s extended scenario of other-than-human realms and that carries along and across those realms the whole human population of London authors and booksellers, all made into matter.[34] A close reading of *The Dunciad* from the perspective of gravity provides a methodology for an analysis of the force of the counterhuman imaginary, exercised despite and against the human. Beginning with an account of the poem's ongoing materialization of human being and next describing the processes by which all of those material objects are gathered, assembled, and entangled in a turbulent state of chaos beyond human convention or law, this chapter accounts for the poem's ultimate, impossible achievement of "a new world to Nature's laws unknown."[35]

Chapter 4, "'When Time Shall End': Poetry of the Lisbon Earthquake," uses the opportunity of the largest earthquake in human history to analyze the literary representation, in the contemporary poetry, of a specific and singular geologic event. On the one hand, these poems can be described as "interchangeable," in that their use of tropes of "disaster discourse"—lists of innumerable human victims—seems to offer only convention, instead of a specific attention to this distinctive event: the other-than-human realm seems to escape human representation. But the evocation of multiplicity itself in these poems offers a starting point for a counterhuman explication. And then, the turn in these poems from a diffuse multiplicity to a powerful, immediate singularity—"the Earthquake *now*!"—points to an other-than-human power that links the earthquake poetry with the coming of "chaos" of *The*

---

34. Alexander Pope, *The Dunciad in Four Books*, in *Poetry and Prose of Alexander Pope*, ed. Aubrey Williams (Boston: Houghton Mifflin, 1969), 4.6.

35. Pope, 3.240.

Dunciad. The ultimate moment of counterhuman uncreation in Pope's poem offers a model for the turn from the many to the momentous in the poetry of the Lisbon earthquake.

Chapter 5 encounters the vast impossibility of the human representation of climate to discover an ongoing crossfire between human authority and unpredictable other-than-human vitality. Chapter 5, "Storms and Torrents: Swift's 'A City Shower' and Defoe's *The Storm*," describes the impact of innumerability and impossibility in both of these distinctive texts. Though the representation of climate is conventionally framed around its impact on human "nature," the "City Shower" and *The Storm* project the experience of weather through forms of confluence and turbulence that move all things and beings indiscriminately, reflecting an agency beyond any human certainty.

This chaotic turbulence and unconventional loving, this irresistible succession of materialities, this sudden turn to a momentous immediacy, and then this creation of an inexpressible, unknowable new world, which these accounts of the other-than-human track across eighteenth-century literary history, taken together offer a view of a diverse and powerful counterhuman imaginary, embedded inextricably in human creativity and emerging necessarily through human discourse and yet projecting an autonomy, agency, force, or even an independence from or repudiation of the human. This is the new paradox that *The Counterhuman Imaginary* presents as a basis for the human critique of the other-than-human. And, paradoxically, the account of the experience of the counterhuman here opens new opportunities to discover manifestations of innovation in human literary culture—innovations that reflect the counterintuitive presence of force, succession, chaos, impossibility, turbulence, and the unknowable, beyond the realm of the human. Human creative innovation arises from the intrusion of the other-than-human and from the impact on human creativity of a realm beyond human accountability and even human understanding.

Figure 1. *Femme nue au chien* (1861–62), by Gustave Courbet. Musée d'Orsay, Paris.

Chapter 1

Species Intimacies

Lapdogs and Banknotes

The counterhuman imaginary presents powerful, corollary scenarios for innovation in the representation of affect in two popular eighteenth-century genres: the circulation narrative and the lapdog lyric. Both place the other-than-human in the role of protagonist—conventionally reserved for human being—and both then offer distinctive challenges relevant to that very notion of human being. The appearance of circulation narratives—or it-narratives—in the mid-eighteenth century has become an engaging topic for literary historians;[1] meanwhile, the sudden currency of lyric poetry focused on lapdogs is a simultaneous, significant generic event in this period. The contiguity between the lapdog lyric and the circulation narrative—in regard to form and affect as well as to their contemporaneity—supplies a

---

1. See Ileana Baird and Christina Ionescu, *Eighteenth-Century Thing Theory in a Global Context: From Consumerism to Celebrity Culture* (Surrey, UK: Ashgate, 2013); Mark Blackwell, ed., *The Secret Life of Things: Animals, Objects, and It-Narratives in Eighteenth-Century England* (Lewisburg, PA: Bucknell University Press, 2007).

perspective both on the nature and also on the innovative potential of the counterhuman imaginary at a particular moment in eighteenth-century literary history. Works in these two genres experiment directly and persistently with the affective connection between the human and the other-than-human—the thing or the animal. Through that experimentation, these literary forms generate an ontological instability arising from the counterhuman discovery of intimacy between beings that are conventionally represented as distinct. Taken together, then, these two generic experiments extend our understanding of the counterhuman imaginary, specifically through its implication with affect. And they suggest that formal literary innovation is at least in part a product of the ontological instability inherent in the experience of the counterhuman.

The lapdog lyric bears witness to a powerful new experiment in the encounter with species difference through the affective representation of the "companion animal"; the circulation narrative reflects an extended engagement with exchange—condensed in the representation of the exchange of hard or bullion coin, commodity money, or, generically, "specie." These superficially distinct subgenres share an ontological problematic that the explication of the counterhuman helps to uncover. "Specie" and "species"—in their origin in the Latin *in specie* or "in kind"—both contain inherent ontological assumptions and thus challenges. In concretizing the value of exchange, "specie" foregrounds the active energy of exchange and the vitality of the material thing, raising the opportunity for a conflation with the energy and vitality assumed to belong to human being. And in designating distinct animal kinds, "species" entails a challenging management of both resemblance and difference, identity and alterity, potentially eluding or eliding the conventional differentiation of the human. An analysis of the contemporaneous and influential literary encounters with "specie" and with "species" in the circulation narrative and the lapdog lyric provides an opportunity to focus on the ontological complexities generated at this moment in eighteenth-century generic history and, in that context, to consider the nature and practice of innovation in literary form—and the distinctive implication of these complexities and innovations with the counterhuman imaginary.

This chapter also engages conceptually with a theoretical topic: the joint implications of the new materialism and of the "affective turn." Taken in tandem, the portrayal of the peripatetic thing-protagonist in the circulation narrative, on the one hand, and of love for the lapdog in the lapdog lyric, on the other, offer a concrete test case for these theoretical "turns." New materialism emphasizes the transformative potential of the actant thing;[2] circulation narrative exemplifies that agency by defying the literary conventions of human-delimited action altogether and portraying a traveling, speaking, acting "it." Affect theory focuses on embodiment and interrelationality;[3] the circulation narrative suffuses its thing-protagonist with human emotion, and the lapdog lyric concretely challenges a disembodied representation of "love" by generating a sustained experiment in the representation of intercorporeality. Things and bodies, actants and affects, together shape a new formal repertory, which this chapter tracks as it emerges from these two distinctive but corollary instances of the counterhuman imaginary.

Eighteenth-century circulation narratives tell the stories of the peregrinations of material things, which move from one human owner or possessor to the next across a self-consciously diverse range of geographical places, cultural situations, and social classes. These stories of circulation adopt the perspective of, for example, an old shoe, a black coat, a goose quill, a sedan, or a cork screw, or a shilling, a bank note, a six-and-nine pence, a silver penny, a rupee, or a guinea. Their popularity in this period, as Aileen Douglas has argued, serves to "register England's transformation into a consumer society."[4] More specifically, they provide for a persistent imaginative focus on modern notions of economic circulation and, through that context, on the status of material things in relation to the realm of sensibility and affect, conventionally ascribed to the human. The relevant context in economic history is familiar. Circulation narrative speaks from and to the significant economic expansion and so-called financial revolution of this period, which sees the

---

2. See for example Diana Coole and Samantha Frost, "Introducing the New Materialisms," in *New Materialisms: Ontology, Agency, and Politics*, ed. Coole and Frost (Durham, NC: Duke University Press, 2010), 1–44; Jane Bennett, *Vibrant Matter: A Political Ecology of Things* (Baltimore: Johns Hopkins University Press, 2010); Christina Ionescu, "Introduction: Through the Prism of Thing Theory: New Approaches to the Eighteenth-Century World of Objects," in Baird and Ionescu, *Eighteenth-Century Thing Theory*, 17–29.

3. See for example Patricia Ticineto Clough, introduction to *The Affective Turn: Theorizing the Social*, ed. Clough and Jean Halley (Durham, NC: Duke University Press, 2007); Lisa Blackman and Couze Venn, "Affect," *Body & Society* 16 (2010): 7–28; Melissa Gregg and Gregory J. Seigworth, "An Inventory of Shimmers," in *The Affect Theory Reader*, ed. Gregg and Seigworth (Durham, NC: Duke University Press, 2010); 1–25; Ruth Leys, "The Turn to Affect: A Critique," *Critical Inquiry* 37 (2010): 434–72; and Marguerite La Caze and Henry Martyn Lloyd, "Editors' Introduction: Philosophy and the 'Affective Turn,'" *Parrhesia* 13 (2011): 1–13.

4. Aileen Douglas, "Britannia's Rule and the It-Narrator," in Blackwell, *Secret Life of Things*, 149.

major growth of commerce, the spread of the commodity, the invention of investment and credit, and the rise of financial speculation, the international money market, and a consumer culture.[5]

This distinctive narrative form is matched by another suddenly—though more briefly—popular poetic subgenre, the lapdog lyric, which also registers another significant contemporary historical transformation: the changed relationship between humans and animals that is visible in the rise of the modern practice of petkeeping. These works directly represent concrete, corporeal ways in which other-than-human beings entered the space and consciousness of human beings in this period, indicating and enacting a major shift in the human-animal relationship and inspiring new forms of cross-species intimacy that we inherit today. Human-animal proximity is a continuous feature of the common history of all beings, but the distinctive cultural practice of petkeeping creates a very specific sort of connection, which recent historians have characterized through such factors as naming, inclusion in the household as a family member, and being endowed with individualist character traits. Thus construed, pets afford alternative opportunities for the experience of affect and intimacy in the newly alienating contexts of modern urbanization. The widespread assumption of intimacy with a companion animal that arose in early eighteenth-century England and that has rapidly expanded from that period to our own is, in Keith Thomas's words, "undoubtedly unique in human history."[6]

Dogs led the pet population in this period, as they do in the present day. More than any other companion animal, dogs provided the complete prototype for the kind of intimacy proposed by the modern idea of petkeeping. Dogs slept with their owners in their beds, ate at their tables, rode in their

---

5. See P. G. M. Dickson, *The Financial Revolution in England: A Study in the Development of Public Credit 1688–1756* (New York: St. Martin's, 1967); John Brewer, *The Sinews of Power: War, Money and the English State, 1688–1783* (New York: Knopf, 1989); Larry Neal, *The Rise of Financial Capitalism: International Capital Markets in the Age of Reason* (Cambridge: Cambridge University Press, 1990).

6. Keith Thomas, *Man and the Natural World: A History of the Modern Sensibility* (New York: Pantheon, 1983), 119. See also Harriet Ritvo, *The Animal Estate: The English and Other Creatures in the Victorian Age* (Cambridge, MA: Harvard University Press, 1987); Ingrid Tague, *Animal Companions: Pets and Social Change in Eighteenth-Century Britain* (University Park: Pennsylvania State University Press, 2015); and Kathleen Kete, *The Beast in the Boudoir: Petkeeping in Nineteenth-Century Paris* (Berkeley: University of California Press, 1994). I have described the literary impact of the invention of petkeeping in *Homeless Dogs and Melancholy Apes: Humans and Other Animals in the Modern Literary Imagination* (Ithaca, NY: Cornell University Press, 2010).

carriages, wore ribbons, feathers, and jewels, and appeared prominently in individual and family portraits. It is in this period that dogs become widely accepted as favored objects of assumptions about animal affection, and they are the first other-than-human beings to be the center of the modern cultural fantasy about companionate intimacy between the human and the other-than-human animal. Thus lapdogs enter on one avenue of literary innovation in this period and the circulation of the material thing enters on another, and they generate converging forms of experimentation around a new literary experience of affection and intimacy that emerges from the challenges generated by the counterhuman imaginary.

I

The prototypical other-than-human protagonist of the circulation narrative is the thing that stands at the heart of contemporary exchange—money, coin, or "specie": a shilling, a bank note, a six-and-nine pence, a silver penny, or a rupee. At the outset of the development of this genre in the first decade of the eighteenth century, Joseph Addison in a *Tatler* essay (1710) provides a thumbnail sketch of the thing that becomes the model protagonist for the genre. In a "most unaccountable reverie" brought on by a friend's reflection on the life of business, which is characterized by ceaseless motion, the Tatler describes how a coin on his bedtable comes to life: "Methoughts the Shilling that lay upon the Table reared it self upon its Edge, and turning the Face towards me, opened its Mouth, and in a soft Silver Sound gave me the following Account of his Life and adventures." This coin then observes, "I found in me a wonderful Inclination to ramble," and proceeds to narrate his own motion "from Hand to Hand . . . into almost every Corner of the Nation."[7]

The story of the circulation of an animated coin reflects the premise of this genre—that exchange confers power and efficacy on the circulating thing itself.[8] And the particular, active character of the coin indicates this

---

7. Joseph Addison, *The Tatler* 249 (November 11, 1710), in *The Tatler*, vol. 3, ed. Donald F. Bond (Oxford, UK: Clarendon, 1987), 269, 270.

8. For an account of the social, cultural, and personal relevance and attributes of exchange media in this period, see Deborah Valenze, *The Social Life of Money in the English Past* (Cambridge: Cambridge University Press, 2006).

narrative's engagement with the nature of being: the coin-protagonist is fully realized as an individual actant in the world of human beings. The first sustained circulation narrative, Charles Gildon's *The Golden Spy* (1709), for example, begins with an assertion on the part of the frame narrator of "the *Sensibility of Things* which we generally not only esteem mute but inanimate" and the access of these things to "Rationality, . . . discursive Faculty, Observation, Memory, and Reflection." And the following pages go on to express the fundamental premise of the circulation narrative as a genre, systematically advancing the Newtonian materialist notion that "ev'ry part of the Universe [is] compos'd of animal sensible, and perhaps rational Particles."[9] Following upon this founding testimony, the story that the golden coin itself then tells reflects this ontological notion in the actions of the coin itself— as it speaks and travels about. And in a corollary way, the coin possesses, by means of its own animation, a seamless integration with and insight into the active as well as the affective properties of human being. The gold piece has an efficacy such that "nothing is more powerful . . . in War, and Peace; in Courts, and Camps; in Church, and State, with the Great and the Fair" and by extension in penetrating the human soul in all its varied physical forms: "Gold would make the Silent speak, and the Loquacious dumb."[10]

Gildon's work is a popular reflection of the contemporary controversy around "thinking matter"—the notion that matter might have actant properties. John Yolton, in his definitive study *Thinking Matter*, describes the widespread influence of John Locke's speculation in the *Essay concerning Human Understanding* that "God could add to matter the power of thought."[11] Canvassing this debate, Yolton invokes Isaac Newton's provocative "Query 31" from the *Opticks*. Here Newton suggests that "the small particles of bodies [have] certain powers virtues or forces by which they act at a distance. . . . It's well known that bodies act one upon another by the attractions of gravity magnetism & electricity, & these instances . . . make it not improbable but that there may be more attractive powers than these."[12] Gildon's coin is thus a lit-

---

9. Charles Gildon, *The Golden Spy* (London: J. Woodward, 1709), 2.

10. Gildon, 2–3.

11. John W. Yolton, *Thinking Matter: Materialism in Eighteenth-Century Britain* (Minneapolis: University of Minnesota Press, 1983), 4.

12. Isaac Newton, "Draft Versions of the Queries (c. 1704–1718)," catalog entry NATP00055, 273r, Newton Project, Cambridge University Library, https://www.newtonproject.ox.uk/. Also cited in Yolton, *Thinking Matter*, 93.

erary enactment of Newton's "subtle Spirit which pervades and lies hid in all gross bodies," in a counterhuman exchange of a thing-protagonist for the conventional human one.[13] But Gildon's narrative reaches beyond the philosophical debate, in popularizing this active and affective thing across a much broader audience and in initiating its long-standing visibility in literary history.

The period's most widely read exemplar of the circulation narrative's materialist focus on specie is Charles Johnstone's *Chrysal; or, The Adventures of a Guinea* (1761). *Chrysal* went through six editions, including significantly expanded versions, between 1761 and 1797. Like Gildon's shilling, Chrysal travels across the economic scenario of western Europe and expresses the contemporary imaginative engagement both with modern concerns of economic exchange and with "thinking matter," in a way that represents the material thing as an active agent and that experiments with the counterhuman potential of the thing to integrate a material form and an affective mode of being.

Johnstone's *Chrysal* demonstrates the ways in which the circulation narrative utilizes specie to create this distinctive imaginative experiment with active, material being. We learn at the outset of Chrysal's story that this narrator / piece of gold was extracted as ore from the earth in a mine in Peru and was from that original material shaped into a gold coin. His discoverer and first owner, aptly surnamed Traffick, is the son of a wealthy London merchant and is "bred . . . to business" but has gone astray through excessive avarice and vanity. The gold coin, Chrysal, is a concretization of the abstract experience of exchange, and as such, the coin participates both in the material substance of the ore and in the power and scope of global economic circulation. Thus the narrative voice, initially that of the speaking piece of gold, merges with the voice or perspective of his first human possessor, Traffick, as the coin describes an ability to "enter into the heart" of the characters he encounters— seamlessly and immediately crossing what would appear to be the absolute boundary between the material thing and the human being. Here is the account of Chrysal's first encounter with Traffick, in Chrysal's own words: "I therefore immediately entered into his heart, to read the events of his life, which I doubted not but I should find deeply imprinted there."[14] Chrysal

---

13. Isaac Newton, *The Mathematical Principles of Natural Philosophy*, vol. 2 (London, 1729), 393. Also cited in Yolton, *Thinking Matter*, 93.

14. Charles Johnstone, *Chrysal; or, The Adventures of a Guinea*, 2 vols. (Dublin: Dillon Chamberlaine, 1760), 1.10, 7. Subsequent references to this source are cited parenthetically in the text.

explains this special power in a full conceptualization of the ability of specie to access human affect:

> And as you may be at a loss, to know how I could arrive at the knowledge of such facts, many of which happened long before my converse with those persons, I shall inform you, that besides that *intuitive knowledge* common to all spirits, we of superior orders, who animate this universal monarch GOLD, have also a power of entering into the hearts of the immediate possessors of our bodies, and there reading all the secrets of their lives. And this will explain to you the cause of that love of gold, which is so remarkable in all who possess any quantity of that metal. (1.5)

The access to human affect that empowers the coin also generates "love" in the possessors of gold; the other-than-human protagonist is both a motive for human action and an intuitive participant in human being. In this way, then, the narrative voice readily melds with the human affect of Traffick, as the gold piece says: "this man . . . as I am *his self*, I shall henceforth, for conciseness and perspicuity, call *my self*" (1.9). What follows then enables the gold piece to provide a direct narrative account of the struggles of Traffick's life in Traffick's own words. And most significant in that narrative is the consistent suffusion of Traffick's story—as told by the gold piece—with affect: the sorrows, regrets, and recollected affinities of Traffick's early years.

This distinctive counterhuman effect of suffusion is pursued consistently throughout Chrysal's story, which is constituted by an almost encyclopedic sequence of owners. The gold coin exercises the same immediate power of access to the direct experiences and sentiments of a range of individuals from gentlemen to beggars, from fashionable ladies to prostitutes, and from Peru to London to Lisbon. Passing from the mine and its owners and tradesmen, Chrysal's next sustained engagement occurs within the confessional, when the other-than-human protagonist comes into the possession of a Catholic priest who is hearing confessions. These interactions—in the confessional itself—between those who are exposing their souls and the (corrupt) priest who is Chrysal's instrument of engagement with them, further foreground the depth of the circulation narrative's access to and suffusion with affective modes of human being.

From the confessional onward, Chrysal's movement through the hands and sentiments of the novel's varied characters unfolds at a pace whose rapidity underscores the persistent integration of matter and affect. Chrysal is cast into a doubloon (1.52) and paid to an English man of war. He makes her way to England, where Chrysal reflects again on the special power of specie to access human subjectivity, a power that makes him both "very different" from and very intimately engaged with human being:

> I must premise to you, that *our* knowledge [the knowledge characteristic of things] is very different from that of men. I have told you, that we know all things *intuitively*, without the trouble, delay, and errors of *discourse* or reasoning. I must now further inform you, that this intuition extends not only to the present face of things, but also has a retrospect to the whole series of their existence, from its first beginning: the *concatenation* between cause and effect being so plain to our eyes, that let us but see any one event of the life of a man, and we immediately know every particular that preceded it. (1.78)

Here the ontological leveling of thing and human being, in its immediacy, even extends to a challenge to human temporality, in the assertion that the guinea's intuition "immediately" transcends time.

Chrysal's efficacy in accessing human existence, as the thing-protagonist then explains, is directly attributable to the status of British specie in European economic exchange; and here the Spanish coin describes his transformation into a guinea—with the consequent affirmation of the "most extensive state" of his power. "I here came into the possession of a new master, and immediately changed my Spanish appearance for the fashion of the country [that is, England], and, in the shape of a guinea, entered into the most extensive state of sublunary influence, becoming the price of every name, that is respected under heaven" (1.77). Once in England, Chrysal passes through the hands of a range of human characters including a noble lord, a virtuoso, an author, "the most celebrated courtesan of the age" (1.122), and a justice of the court. The coin encounters many people at a charity feast, including a gentleman and lady of high life, a servant, and a general, and travels between London and Lisbon, among societies and companies military, aristocratic, female, criminal, judicial, religious, and occult. The specificity of human beings in this sequence underscores the local, bodily, delimited nature of merely human being, in contrast to the counterhuman scope of the other-than-human, which implicitly claims a much broader scenario of engagement than any human can compass.

In the course of the narrative, the other-than-human protagonist exposes the affections of each of the encountered individuals through the extensive scope of the coin's "sublunary influence," its unique form of intuitive knowledge, and its distinctive access to core aspects of human affect. By this means, specie—the material concretization of economic exchange—is directly correlated with an unmediated convergence with human being and thus with a kind of transcendence of all human beings. The thing-protagonist ends the adventures of the second volume in the hands of the human frame narrator, the "master," who is on the verge of receiving through the necessary mediation of Chrysal "the *occult wisdom* . . . which links the animal and the material worlds together" (2.218). That revelation fails, due to the insuppressible bodily impulse of the human coin-holder. Thus, in the narrative's last scene, the "consummation of human knowledge" offered by specie vanishes forever (2.219), leaving this text ironically failing to fulfill what had promised to be a full convergence of human and other-than-human being— ultimately an impossibility.

That such an impossible convergence is an ongoing opportunity and even a premise of the circulation narrative is emphasized in the early development of the subgenre in the middle decades of the eighteenth century. The circulation narrative in this formative period is dominated by narratives that place the human being in a physical proximity with the narrator-object: the human either wears or is installed upon or within the nonhuman narrator. The relevant works include *The Secret History of an old Shoe* (1734), *The Sopha* (Claude Crébillon, 1742), *The Settee* (1742), *The Adventures of a Black Coat* (Edward Philips, 1750), *The Memoirs and Interesting Adventures of an Embroidered Waistcoat* (1751), *The Stage-Coach* (1753), *Travels of Mons. Le Post-Chaise* (1753), *The History and Adventures of a Lady's Slippers and Shoes* (1754), and *The Sedan* (1757).[15]

That latter narrative—*The Sedan: A Novel: In Which Many New and Entertaining Characters are Introduced*—exemplifies repeatedly this premise of physical proximity that generates the affective convergence of human and thing that we have seen to be at stake in *Chrysal*. For *The Sedan*, of course, the proximity of the sedan-narrator to the human is materially generated by

---

15. For the complete "Chronological Catalogue of Circulation Narratives," see Liz Bellamy, "It-Narrators and Circulation: Defining a Subgenre," in Blackwell, *Secret Life of Things*, appendix B, 135.

the enclosed and private physical environment of the sedan chair, which accommodates one person. The sedan-narrator—after briefly establishing their "furnishing" and "finishing" in "a shop somewhere on Leicester-street"— "issues forth," arrives at the stand where potential passengers convene, and begins a seriatim account of the intimate confidences of a series of customers or "visitors" whose confessions and revelations and speculations make up two volumes of sequential vignettes of human affect—from politics to poetry to romance—in which the sedan-narrator is a direct and immediate auditor-plus-participant.[16] The sedan-narrator voices the revelations of these passengers in the first person, as if the material proximity of the enclosed physical space makes such an immediacy natural or necessary. In some chapters, this intimacy between the sedan-narrator and the passenger is explicitly described as a conversation: "she amus'd me with some anecdotes of some private families" (1.8). Sometimes the sedan-narrator represents the revelation of their passenger as overheard: "But little thinking I had the faculty of hearing, she whispered" (1.9). And at some points the words of the passenger are represented by the sedan-narrator as a straightforward, deliberate confidence: "What followed I had from his own lips" (1.30). As the narrative proceeds, one of the human sedan-bearers, Paddy, is included as a corollary interlocutor alongside the sedan-narrator, but his role only augments the sedan-narrator's primacy in engaging in these intimacies. Throughout *The Sedan*, the boundary between the sedan-auditor and their human confidant is ambiguous or flexible or—most often—nonexistent. Here the full, five-page inner life of a hypocritical Methodist clergyman—"our first fare this morning"—emerges naturally and immediately upon his entrance into the space of the sedan chair:

> He had scarce entered and sat down but he began—Well, as my old friend Shakespear says, though I dare not now read him in publick, *all the world's a stage, and all the men and women merely players*. Bishops, deans, and dignitaries, may laugh if they will, but the homage we have is more than ever their paltry feathers can command—we have it . . . as high as the church of Rome; and as to income, I declare I would not change with the dean of St Paul's; . . . I do declare I starved till I fell into this method. Now I have twenty invitations

---

16. *The Sedan: A Novel*, 2 vols. (London: R. Baldwin, 1757), 1.3–5. Subsequent references to this source are cited parenthetically in the text.

in a day to dine, and, though we preach abstinence, we eat as well as the bench of bishops. . . . But I see we are near arrived; I must rub my eyes to make them look weak, as if with much affliction for the sins of mankind, or much reading for their good. (1.155–59)

These confessional words belong as much to the sedan-chair-narrator as to the human passenger; the discursive convergence of human and thing is pervasive in this narrative, enacting that suffusion of matter and affect, and that ontological leveling of thing and human being, that defines the counterhuman form of the circulation narrative.

II

Aside from specie—the prototypical guinea, shilling, or rupee—the circulation narrative has another prototypical protagonist, the animal: a parrot, a cat, a mouse, a canary, a hare, a little pony, and others, including, most famously, a lapdog. Published in the same decade as *Chrysal*, Francis Coventry's *The History of Pompey the Little, or the Life and Adventures of a Lapdog* (1751) was an immensely popular novel that went to a third edition within the year of its initial publication and was widely read through the first quarter of the nineteenth century. By 1824, *Pompey the Little* had seen at least ten English editions, two Dublin piracies, and a French and an Italian translation.[17] Coventry's *Pompey the Little* is not only the century's most visible circulation narrative but also the first widely read modern dog narrative. In the nineteenth century, the animal narrator comes to dominate the circulation narrative, and this animal-protagonist circulation story continues as a popular narrative form into the twenty-first century.

The guinea and the pet, then, are the two primary protagonists of the circulation narrative for eighteenth-century readers. The equivalency of the thing and the lapdog that is suggested by this concurrence uncovers a conjunction between the imaginative engagement with "specie" and with "species": both propose ontological challenges around autonomy and identity, and both

---

17. Robert Adams Day, introduction to *The History of Pompey the Little*, by Francis Coventry (London: Oxford University Press, 1974), xiv. Subsequent references to the novel are cited parenthetically in the text.

experiment across the boundaries of the human and the other-than-human. In fact, in this period, as Wolfgang Schmidgen demonstrates, the term "species" itself referred broadly across material things and animate beings, putting into semantic play those ontological challenges referenced in each of these terms separately.[18] Thus, when the lapdog occupies the place of the guinea as the protagonist of circulation, the power of specie that we have already canvassed in *Chrysal* is aligned with the imaginative challenge of species difference.

The dog-protagonist of *Pompey* demonstrates the same counterhuman power as the thing-protagonist of *Chrysal*—to penetrate human affect wherever it is found. Pompey is born in Bologna and raised in the home of a "celebrated Courtesan" (7); his early adventures first demonstrate his close affinity with his female mistresses. He is given to a fashionable gentleman on his grand tour who takes him to England—in a transnational transfer typical of the circulation genre—and presents him to his mistress, Lady Tempest. There, Pompey "becomes a Dog of the Town, and shines in High-life," attending Lady Tempest everywhere—to the playhouse and the opera, even learning "to play at Cards" (30). In these episodes, the lapdog's special engagement with the woman are decisively highlighted. In fact, Pompey's connection with her Ladyship is so close that he shares, at her side, the prototypical site of the female fashionable world, and "in less than three Months . . . sit[s] down with her Ladyship to Piquet" (31).

Pompey then moves from the world of fashion to the City; he is passed to an innkeeper and then to a blind beggar who travels with him to Bath. Like Chrysal's movements, these changes introduce various human portraits—of the world of high fashion, bourgeois social climbing, marriage, Methodism, usury, and coffeehouse conversation—whose intimacies Pompey readily penetrates. Finally, Pompey returns to fashionable life, as he is given to a pair of good-natured sisters, sold to a prosperous widow milliner, stolen by a Lord, given to a penniless poet, and then passed to a Cambridge scholar. Pompey's perspective opens up an inclusive scope of human affects and affections—female folly, doctors, lawyers, modern science, education and pedantry, and poetry and the contemporary theater. Finally, Pompey returns to the world of women when he is rediscovered by his original mistress, Lady Tempest, where, in his fourteenth year, he is "gathered to the Lapdogs of Antiquity" (200).

---

18. Wolfram Schmidgen, "The Metaphysics of *Robinson Crusoe*," *ELH* 83 (2016): 104.

At all points in these peregrinations, the dog-protagonist's animal status offers a direct opportunity for ontological questioning about the nature of being and for specific reflection on species boundaries, which make explicit the counterhuman boundary-crossing that we saw portrayed in the thing-protagonist's penetration of the human heart. This specific reflection is expressed on two occasions in Coventry's story of the lapdog. First, one night Pompey accompanies one of his masters to a tavern, where his presence inspires a heated debate on animals' capacity for reason. The freethinker in the group advances a current, challenging boundary-crossing argument: that animals are capable of reasoning and morality. He summarizes, "I have a curious thesis now by me, . . . those dogs there put me in the head of it. . . . I undertake to prove that brutes think and have intellectual faculties. . . . I go farther . . . and maintain that they are reasonable creatures, and moral agents" (171). The other participant, a parson, then counters with the conventional theological defense of the uniqueness of the human soul—a uniqueness based on the idea of the human participation in the divine. In this context, both the parson and the freethinker are objects of ridicule, but their extended discussion reproduces one of the central ontological debates of the period, into which *Pompey the Little* explicitly inserts itself.

And earlier in Pompey's travels, the topic of species difference and boundary crossing is raised through another debate. Lady Sophister, arguing with two physicians on the topic of the immortality of the soul, makes use of a sketch of Locke's idea of matter to summarize a current strain of thinking that directly engages the problem of species difference and that of the status of the material thing, at once:

> Mr. *Locke* observes, there are various kinds of matter. . . . *Matter* . . . is an extended solid Substance— . . . out of this matter some . . . is made into roses and peach-trees; then the next step which matter takes, is animal life; from whence you know we have lions and elephants, and all the race of brutes. Then the last step, as Mr. *Locke* observes, is thought and reason and volition, from whence are created men, and therefore you very plainly see, 'tis impossible for the soul to be immortal. (37)

Their argument ultimately turns to Pompey himself, whom Lady Sophister cites as an immediate example of her case:

"You say, I think, Sir, . . . that a multitude of opinions will establish a truth. [This would be the multitude of opinions supporting the immateriality of the human soul, which the physician has just cited.] Now you know all the *Indians* believe that their dogs will go to heaven along with them; and if a great many opinions can prove any thing to be true, what say you to that, Sir? [In other words, that absurdity should call into question his rejection of materialism. And she adds,] . . . For instance, now, there's lady *Tempest*'s little lapdog" [as a way of emphasizing the absurdity of the argument based on a multitude of opinions and of implying that one certainly could not accept the heathen notion that a little lapdog like Pompey could go to heaven, no matter how many Indians believe it. And then Lady Tempest counters]—"My dear little creature," said lady *Tempest*, catching him up in her arms, "will you go to heaven along with me? I shall be vastly glad of your company, *Pompey*, if you will." (39)

Lady Tempest is here both asserting and physically demonstrating a cross-species affinity, which reaches across a challenging, categorical boundary through the explicit evocation of affect. This episode from *Pompey the Little* reveals the corollary positions of species difference and specie in the counterhuman imaginary of the circulation narrative. The pet and the material thing coincide here, as equivalent other-than-human reference points both for difference from and then for intimacy with the human.

These instances from *Pompey the Little* anchor the circulation narrative in a visible intellectual context—that of the vital contemporary engagement with theological, ontological, and scientific ideas both about species difference and about materiality and immateriality. In the realm of species difference, a range of debates can be identified as they emerge through ongoing adjustments in the hierarchical conceptualization of the Platonistic chain of being: new thinking on the topics of animal intelligence, language, and anatomy supported revisions in those concepts in which the principles of continuity and plenitude began to take precedence over doctrinal notions of the separation of human from other-than-human beings and of other-than-human beings from matter. Closely related to these developments was the debate about animal souls, in which the Cartesian analogy between animal and automaton—decisively distinguishing man from beast in this regard—met with dispute from a range of perspectives, including the arguments of rationalizing theology and the rise of the new humanitarianism.[19] Meanwhile, and along corollary routes, Enlightenment materialism developing from Descartes and from Lockean empiricism, from the experimental practices and discourse of the British Royal Society, and from the influential European and French metaphysical debates proposed a continuity along and throughout the chain of being that extended to the matter of its first stage. Coventry's novel places the circulation narrative explicitly within these contemporary discussions of difference—between human and other-than-human beings.

III

These occasions in which other-than-human modes of being encounter or challenge or exceed the human through the evocation of affect or intimacy can be further illuminated through a comparison between the circulation narrative and the corollary subgenre that we reviewed at the outset of this chapter—the lapdog lyric. As we have seen, as a distinctive generic innovation, the circulation narrative is invented alongside the lapdog lyric in the early part of the eighteenth century; the juxtaposition of these two genres extends our understanding both of the imaginative status and of the formal function of affect and intimacy in the counterhuman imaginary. *Pompey the Little* supplies a direct link to the lapdog lyric. As the preceding summary suggests, Pompey's affective insights highlight women and the supposed sexual excesses that are central to the eighteenth-century stereotypes of female petkeeping. The lapdog's immoderate intimacy with the woman of quality is a prominent dimension of *Pompey the Little*: a recurring scene in this narrative is the appearance of the lapdog in an intimate connection with a lady

---

19. For an account of the debate about animal souls, see Thomas, *Man and the Natural World*, 139–42; and Christine Kenyon-Jones, *Kindred Brutes: Animals in Romantic-Period Writing* (Aldershot, UK: Ashgate, 2001), 15–27. For a thumbnail summary of the religious arguments regarding animal souls and of the developing new ideas of humanity, see David Perkins, *Romanticism and Animal Rights* (Cambridge: Cambridge University Press, 2003), 27–41. For the French theriophilist movement of the period, which was influential in England, see George Boas, *The Happy Beast in French Thought of the Seventeenth Century* (1933; repr., New York: Octagon Books, 1966). Ingrid H. Tague describes the treatment of animal souls and of metempsychosis in pet epitaphs, concluding that "the view that animals might have immortal souls like humans was not that of the majority, but ideas that stopped short of this position were common." Tague, "Dead Pets: Satire and Sentiment in British Elegies and Epitaphs for Animals," *Eighteenth-Century Studies* 42 (2008): 299.

of fashion. For example, here is Pompey in the embrace of the fashionable lady, Aurora, with whom "he was a great favourite. . . . *Aurora* . . . caressed him with the fondest tenderness, and permitted him to sleep every night in a chair by her bed-side. When she awoke in a morning, she would embrace him with an ardour, which the happiest lover might have envied" (132). Aurora's "ardour" is a direct allusion to the innovative engagement with cross-species intimacy that is at the center of the lapdog lyric. Pompey's narrative explores the counterhuman impact of ontological leveling across an extended narrative scenario. But the lapdog lyric takes up this engagement with intimacy especially intensively and almost exclusively, through a focused format that develops in a concentrated generic movement in the first three decades of the eighteenth century.

The lapdog lyric is consumed with the problematic of the lady's love for her favorite lapdog. These poems include a range of ironic tributes—from epitaphs and praise poems to satiric, envious reflections on the favorite lapdog, who is inevitably preferred to the husband or suitor. All across this genre, certain key images indicate these works' contribution to a common, developing discourse of embodied cross-species connection—images focused on the lapdog's proximity with the woman, her dress and accoutrements, her breasts and thighs. These poems can become investigations of a surprising cross-species intimacy, usually expressed as a sexual connection.

In the circulation narrative, the challenge of the other-than-human is a destabilizing force. The peripatetic activity of the thing-narrator as it operates across the globe and across the social strata, together with the power of this narrator to engage and expose the most intimate affections of human being, emphasizes the counterhuman disruption of conventional expectations around the necessity for a human actor and around the human specificity of affect. In the lapdog lyric as well, the challenge of the other-than-human generates ontological instability—based in this case on cross-species transposition or substitution and on a corollary sense of immeasurability represented through the corporeality of the woman-lapdog intimacy.

Corporeality and female sexuality are the implicit and explicit conditions of this poetry's evocation of cross-species intimacy. The lapdog lyric alludes, on the one hand, to the early modern *blazon anatomique*, best characterized by John Donne's "The Flea"—where the animal enables a direct physical and aesthetic exploration of the female body—and on the other hand to the classical topos of the dead pet, where animal mortality serves as a pretext for the portrayal and exploitation of female affective excess. In the lapdog lyric, the animal is often named as the lady's "bedfellow," and the venue of this poetry is consistently depicted as the female bed.[20] The opening scene of Alexander Pope's *Rape of the Lock* (1714), for instance, famously places Belinda in her bed dreaming of her lovers—with the lapdog Shock, "who thought she slept too long, [and] / Leapt up, and wak'd his Mistress with his Tongue."[21]

The lady's "lap" creates the same venue for corporeal contact. Jonathan Smedley's "On the Death of a Lap-Dog" (1723) describes the typical scene:

> To him her softest things she'd say:
> Oft on her downy Breast he lay;
> And oft he took a gentle Nap,
> Upon her Sleep-inticing Lap.[22]

Isaac Thompson's "The Lap-Dog" (1731) describes this scene as well:

> Securely on her Lap it lies,
> Or freely gazes on her Eyes;
> To touch her Breast, may share the Bliss,
> And unreprov'd, may snatch a Kiss.[23]

And this intimacy is often extended to an explicit portrayal of sexual contact. "An Epitaph upon my Lady M——'s Lapdog" (1731) portrays an embodied cross-species intimacy directly:

> Beneath this Stone, ah woful Case!
> Poor little *Doxy* lies,
> Who once possess'd a warmer Place
> Between his Lady's T——hs.[24]

---

20. For instance, a contemporary letter of condolence, "To a Lady on the Death of her Lapdog and Squirrel in One Day," describes "little *Dory*" as having "the charmingest Creature in the World for his Bedfellow." In *Serious and Comical Chapters* (London: J. King, 1710), letter 16, 180.

21. Alexander Pope, *The Rape of the Lock*, in *Poetry and Prose of Alexander Pope*, ed. Aubrey Williams (Boston: Houghton Mifflin, 1969), 1.115–16.

22. Jonathan Smedley, *Poems on Several Occasions* (London, 1723), 122.

23. Isaac Thompson, *A Collection of Poems* (Newcastle upon Tyne, 1731), 94.

24. Mr. Bavius, *The Grub-Street Miscellany* (London: J. Wilford, 1731), 45.

The Rival Lapdog and the Tale (1730) develops a full account of an embodied cross-species connection. This work tells the story of a King Charles spaniel who "was *Courtly-bred*": "*Court-Company* he always kept, / With *Lords* he din'd, with Ladies slept."[25] His "monst'rous" act is to supplant his lord in his lady's bed. He takes "*saucy Freedoms*" (8) with his lady's belongings and her clothes, but beyond that, he is seen to "towze Her, with his Paw," while the lady in turn "*was proud to have her dear Dog rude, / As rude with Her, as e'er He cou'd*" (36). The poem climaxes with a sustained interspecies love scene:

> *Breast to Breast*, incorporate
> Almost, He lay like *Dog in State*;
> . . . .
> *Fair-Lady*, all in Raptures, to
> Be so *caress'd* by *such a Beau*;
> She hugg'd, and kiss'd, and cry'd, and clung,
> And He return'd all with his Tongue;
> Put *Lady-Fair* quite out of Breath,
> And buss't her, *e'en a'most* to Death;
> *Sir Lick Lips* was so *tir'd* too,
> He fell a sleep while *One* tell's *Two*. (39)

The typical transposition here, of dog for lord, signals this poetry's persistent disruption of ontological stability. For instance, "On a Lap-Dog" (Thomas Brown, 1721) addresses the dog with this exclamation: "Nice, pretty Nice, . . . ah! Could'st thou know / How thou dost my Envy raise." Then as the dog lies in "that Lap," the speaker asks his mistress whether she will consider an "Exchange" of "Place" and "Station" so that the dog's "Privilege" will instead be his.[26] "The Lap-Dog" (Isaac Thompson, 1731) goes further, by proposing a magical transformation:

> Give me a Spell, a potent Charm,
> To turn myself to MINNY's form!
> In sportful Dance, and wanton Play
> On *Silvia*'s Lap I'll spend the Day.[27]

---

25. [Stephen Fox?], *The Rival Lapdog and the Tale* (London: W. Smith and G. Greg, 1730), 7. Subsequent references to this source are cited parenthetically in the text.

26. Thomas Brown, *The Fifth Volume of the Works of Mr. Thomas Brown* (London: Sam. Briscoe, 1721), 333.

27. Thompson, *Collection of Poems*, 94.

John Hewitt's "Upon Cælia's having a little Dog in her Lap" (1727) expresses a clear preference—to be a "four-footed" being rather than a man:

> 'Tis four-footed *Cloe*, your Smiles can engage,
> Whilst a Shape that is human must bear with your Rage,
> Since, thus, my Addresses by *Cælia*'s refused,
> Pray, who wou'd be Man? when a Dog's so well us'd?[28]

The speaker wishes himself into the animal's place—and the animal into the human's place—in a way that engages with contemporary debates around human rationality, animal souls, and being itself. Transposition or even transformation is an ongoing theme, as this poetry posits a multiply directed counterhuman experiment in simultaneous intimacy and alterity. The dog is both close and distant, both a source of a special intimacy with the lady and a problematic or unnatural or negative model for affective connection.

Both multiplicity and transformation shape the definition of love in Henry Carey's "The Rival Lap-Dog" (1713), where the male suitor issues a complaint to the lady that takes the form of a rhetorical question that is further evocative of a complex cross-species connection:

> Corinna, pray tell me,
> When thus you repel me,
> When humbly I sue for a Kiss,
>   Why *Dony*, at pleasure,
>   May kiss without measure,
> And surfeit himself with the Bliss?[29]

Again, the male speaker is both a jealous observer of cross-species "bliss" and a critic- competitor, implicitly presenting his unsuccessful intraspecies suit as the preferable form of intimacy. The "pleasure/measure" rhyme in this poem, exemplifying and extending "kiss/bliss," places "pleasure" in an unstable—even disruptive—relationship to all the participants: the woman and the lapdog, as well as the male observer or would-be lover. Though "pleasure" and "bliss" refer grammatically to Dony's experience, these words

---

28. John Hewitt, *Miscellanies in Prose and Verse* (Bristol, UK: Penn, 1727), 29.
29. Henry Carey, *Poems on Several Occasions* (London: J. Kent, A Boulter, and J. Brown, 1713), 25.

point also to the imputed pleasure of the female recipient of these cross-species kisses, as well as the projected pleasure of the intraspecies suitor with his imagined kiss. In this context, the indication that this experience of embodied affect is "without measure" registers its disruptive and challenging form. The lapdog lyric is characterized by these counterhuman formal structures—where difference is superseded by connection, where transformation problematizes hierarchy as well as alterity, where pleasure is multiply determined, and where the outcome is represented as an unexpected and "unmeasurable," and even—from the human perspective—inexplicable or impossible, affect.

IV

These two genres—the circulation narrative and the lapdog lyric—constitute corollary, contemporary, sustained innovations in eighteenth-century literary history that arise directly from the representation of other-than-human being and the incursion of a counterhuman imaginary through or alongside that representation. We have seen the local and the conceptual connections between these genres, in their evocation of contemporary debates around the definition of the human in relationship to the other-than-human. And we have also seen, derived from their engagement with the challenge of the other-than-human, their mutual attempts to design new modes of imaginative engagement with action, affect, and affinity, which step beyond or outside conventional or human agency or connection—generating instability along corollary pathways.

In the one case—the circulation narrative—this experiment in creating an active thing-protagonist opens up the surprising possibility that the material thing or specie—in possessing access to and in melding with human affect—might itself represent a mode of being equivalent to that of the human. In this regard, the circulation narrative offers an experiment in materialist form that shows how the literary imagination both shapes and is shaped by a material actant. In the other case—the lapdog lyric—the experiment in cross-species corporeal intimacy challenges or multiplies or destabilizes conventional notions and representations of affinity. Based on embodied cross-species intimacy, a new definition of affect emerges as a result—a definition based on multiplicity and immeasurability rather than identity and coherence, and on a fundamental questioning of a human-dominated and exclusively human affectivity. In this context, embodied affect advances formal innovation by providing an imaginative site for transposition. These two genres address fundamental challenges around matter and affect that are posed by the experience of modernity. They place human being into surprising, direct, intimate contact with the other-than-human. This contact propels the imaginative experience both of matter and of affect beyond the bounds of convention and creates the opportunity for a new and vital framework in which ideas about efficacy and intimacy, and about being itself, may be reimagined. The counterhuman imaginary is the enactment of this reimagining.

Figure 2. *Jar* (1857), by David Drake. Yale University Art Gallery.

Chapter 2

ACTIVE MATTER, VITAL FORCE

Newton and Defoe

Daniel Defoe's *Robinson Crusoe* (1719) and Isaac Newton's "Queries" to the *Optics* (1704, 1717–18, 1730), taken jointly, can be used to characterize a turning point in the modern encounter with matter. Viewed together, these texts define a key moment at which certain powerful formal forces distinctive to the counterhuman imaginary are foregrounded for contemporary readers and for current new materialist critics. "Things" have become a fertile topic for literary critics, producing various distinctive definitions of "matter." The range of these definitions suggests the vitality generated by and implicit in the topic, for modern readers—a vitality predicted in the eighteenth century by *Robinson Crusoe* and the *Optics*.

In Jonathan Lamb's account in *The Things Things Say*, the thing is entirely removed from the human—to be understood as "things purely as they are." According to Lamb, these "pure" things "disturb" literary texts because they are "obstinately solitary, superficial, and self-evident, sometimes in flight but not in our direction; they communicate only with themselves and have no value in the market that they reckon."[1] For Jane Bennett, on the other hand, far from being removed or "solitary," the thing is "vitally" engaged and efficacious. Bennett's enabling quality is "thing-power," and its impact is transferrable, in that "attentiveness to (nonhuman) things and their powers can have a laudable effect on humans."[2] For Diana Coole and Samantha Frost, in their introduction to *New Materialisms: Ontology, Agency, and Politics*, the emphasis is specifically ontological—extending beyond "vitality" to the actual agency of matter: "material forces themselves manifest . . . agentic capacities," which are "active, self-creative, productive" and which require the "rethinking of the whole edifice of modern ontology . . . regarding change, causality, agency."[3] And distinctively, for Ileana Baird and Christina Ionescu in their introductions to *Eighteenth-Century Thing Theory in a Global Context*, the challenge presented by the eighteenth-century thing resides in its "multifarious array of functions"—exemplified by the range of thing-protagonists in the "so-called 'it narrative'" that arises in midcentury. The singular defining quality of things, then, from Baird and Ionescu's perspective, becomes movement; things may be extraordinarily diverse, but their common denominator is exchangeability or circulation. Thus their impact is generated through their "global peregrinations": things create "relational maps" and "more expansive geographies."[4]

These statements offer a small sample of the scope of current interpretations of the nature and role of matter: "things" might indicate obstinate solitude, a vital efficacy, an "agentic" force, or expansive global movement. These things might disrupt or undermine human structures of communication or expression; they might efficaciously merge their powers with the forces of human activity; they might act on their own with a force equivalent

---

1. Jonathan Lamb, *The Things Things Say* (Princeton, NJ: Princeton University Press, 2011), xii, xi.

2. Jane Bennett, "The Force of Things: Steps toward an Ecology of Matter," *Political Theory* 32 (2004): 348.

3. Diana Coole and Samantha Frost, "Introducing the New Materialisms," in *New Materialisms: Ontology, Agency, and Politics*, ed. Coole and Frost (Durham, NC: Duke University Press, 2010), 8, 9.

4. Ilena Baird, "Introduction: Peregrine Things: Rethinking the Global in Eighteenth-Century Studies," in *Eighteenth-Century Thing Theory in a Global Context: From Consumerism to Celebrity Culture*, ed. Baird and Ionescu (Farnham, UK: Ashgate, 2013), 1–16; and Christina Ionescu, "Introduction: Through the Prism of Thing Theory," in *Eighteenth-Century Thing Theory*, 17–30. Quotations are from Baird, "Introduction," 14, 12, 8, 3, 8.

to or expansive of the category of being; or they might level and renegotiate global structures and processes by crossing geographical and temporal boundaries.[5] This profusion of meanings can be managed through a grounding analysis of the formal features of the counterhuman imaginary, with specific reference to Defoe's and Newton's discourse. The impact of matter in *Robinson Crusoe* and the *Optics* exemplifies and demonstrates the counterintuitive and contrapuntal status of matter for the modern human imagination. Given the concrete, local nature of the thing itself, the challenges that matter presents to literary critique are best addressed concretely or inductively: from the core moment of the portrayal of matter, objects, and "things" onward toward the recognition of materialism's status in the literary history of modernity and the broader conceptualization of materialism's impact as a method of literary critique. Explicating the formal dimensions of the representation of matter in these two works creates the opportunity to develop a counterhumanist methodology.

I

Defoe's *Robinson Crusoe* and Newton's speculative writing on the forces of gravitation in his "Queries" to the *Optics* are the iconic portrayals of matter for our time. From their own age onward, the contribution of these texts to the status of the "thing" has been widely visible: readers have understood that Newton "was trying to reshape the entire conception of matter" and

---

5. See for example Jane Bennett, *Vibrant Matter: A Political Ecology of Things* (Durham, NC: Duke University Press, 2010); Baird, "Introduction"; Ionescu, "Introduction"; Bill Brown, "Thing Theory," *Critical Inquiry* 28 (2001): 1–22; Bill Brown, ed., *Things: A Critical Inquiry Book* (Chicago: University of Chicago Press, 2004); Coole and Frost, "Introducing the New Materialisms." Meanwhile, critical analysis of description per se and of the appearance of objects—especially in eighteenth- and nineteenth-century literature—continues to deepen our formal engagement with this topic; for example Lynn Festa, "Crusoe's Island of Misfit Things," *The Eighteenth Century* 52 (2011): 443–71; Elaine Freedgood, *The Ideas in Things: Fugitive Meaning in the Victorian Novel* (Chicago: University of Chicago Press, 2006); Cynthia Wall, *The Prose of Things: Transformations of Description in the Eighteenth Century* (Chicago: University of Chicago Press, 2006); Mark Blackwell, ed., *The Secret Life of Things: Animals, Objects, and It-Narratives in Eighteenth-Century England* (Lewisburg, PA: Bucknell University Press, 2007); Julie Park, *The Self and It: Novel Objects and Material Subjects in Eighteenth-Century England* (Stanford, CA: Stanford University Press, 2009); Bill Brown, *A Sense of Things: The Object Matter of American Literature* (Chicago: University of Chicago Press, 2004).

that *Robinson Crusoe* represents for literary history "an expression of modern materialism."[6] These texts inspire and enact a redefinition of the material world—one for the new science and the other for the new imaginative experience of literary realism.

In the case of *Robinson Crusoe*, we are in the presence of the most often redacted imaginative work of the modern period. The recent film *The Martian* (2015) demonstrates the currency of Defoe's representation of the "castaway" (Matt Damon), the "desert island" (Mars), and the compelling assemblage of things that come to populate an "empty" landscape. The label "robinsonade" was coined in 1731 by Johann Gottfried Schnabel in his preface to *Die Insel Felsenburg*, but this subgenre had its inception immediately, in the year after the publication of *Robinson Crusoe*, with the publication in 1720 of the *Voyages, Dangerous Adventures, and Imminent Escapes of Captain Richard Falconer.*[7] Across a range of scenarios—from survival, labor, production, accumulation, economic agency, children's literature, and even homemaking—*Robinson Crusoe*'s immersion in the realm of objects has drawn modern readers to its imaginative world. For example, even in the context of children's literature, where adventure would seem to be the source of attraction, instead the world of objects presides: *Robinson Crusoe* can be seen as supporting or even helping to establish an educational theory of experiential learning, which promoted "fictions *about* direct experience of the object world."[8]

In the discipline of economics, immediately emergent in the decades following the novel's publication, the engagement with *Robinson Crusoe* begins with David Hume and Adam Smith, then famously includes Karl Marx, and extends to the present day. A recent collection of essays—*Robinson Crusoe's Economic Man* (2011)—continuing the novel's visibility among economists and advancing the development of this field of study—"uses the device of Robinson Crusoe to contribute to a genealogy of economic agency and a cri-

---

6. Ernan McMullin, *Newton on Matter and Energy* (Notre Dame, IN: University of Notre Dame Press, 1979), 43; Wolfram Schmidgen, "The Metaphysics of *Robinson Crusoe*," *ELH* 83 (2016): 101.

7. Andrew O'Malley, *Children's Literature, Popular Culture, and Robinson Crusoe* (New York: Palgrave Macmillan, 2012), 48. For this context, see also Michael V. White, "The Production of an Economic *Robinson Crusoe*," in *Robinson Crusoe's Economic Man: A Construction and Deconstruction*, ed. Ulla Grapard and Gillian Hewitson (New York: Routledge, 2011); originally published in *Southern Review* 15 (1982): 115–42.

8. Alan Richardson, *Literature, Education, and Romanticism: Reading as Social Practice, 1780–1832* (Cambridge: Cambridge University Press, 1994), 132; cited in O'Malley, *Children's Literature*, 29.

tique of the discipline of economics."[9] *Robinson Crusoe* has been cited in conceptualizations of instrumental rationality, of labor and value and the nature of their connection, and of the *homo economicus*—for which Crusoe is the model. Marx, most significantly, uses *Robinson Crusoe* to illustrate the labor theory of value, crediting the long-standing role of the novel for theorists on this topic—"Crusoe's experiences are a favourite theme with political economists":

> [Crusoe] knows that his labour, whatever its form, is but the activity of one and the same Robinson, and consequently, that it consists of nothing but different modes of human labour. . . . This our friend Robinson soon learns by experience, and having rescued a watch, ledger, and pen and ink from the wreck, commences, like a true-born Briton, to keep a set of books. His stockbook contains a list of the objects of utility that belong to him, of the operations necessary for their production; and lastly, of the labour time that definite quantities of those objects have, on an average, cost him. All the relations between Robinson and the objects that form this wealth of his own creation, are here so simple and clear as to be intelligible without exertion. . . . And yet those relations contain all that is essential to the determination of value.[10]

Ian Watt brought the "Robinson Crusoe Economy (RCE)" into the canonical literary critical conceptualization of the rise of the novel, by highlighting Crusoe's established status as an economic paradigm:[11]

> [Defoe] takes his hero to a primitive environment, where labour can be presented as varied and inspiring, and . . . there is an absolute equivalence between individual effort and individual reward, . . . [thus enabling] Defoe to give narrative expression to the ideological counterpart of the Division of Labour, the Dignity of Labour. . . . *Robinson Crusoe* is certainly the first novel in the sense that it is the first fictional narrative in which an ordinary person's daily activities are the centre of continuous literary attention. . . . The dignity of labour helped to bring into being the novel's general premise that the

---

9. Ulla Grapard, Gillian Hewitson, "Introduction: Economics and Literature," in Grapard and Hewitson, *Robinson Crusoe's Economic Man*, 5.

10. Karl Marx, *Capital*, trans. Samuel Moore and Edward Aveling (1906; repr., Mineola, NY: Dover, 2011), 88.

11. "Robinson Crusoe Economy" is Michael V. White's coinage in "The Production of an Economic Robinson Crusoe."

individual's daily life is of sufficient importance and interest to be the proper subject of literature.[12]

Watt connects the novel's distinctive portrayal of labor with Calvinist individualism and introspective discipline; the eighteenth-century secularization of Puritan ideology explains *Robinson Crusoe*'s canonical role in the rise of the novel. But, Watt concedes, "Defoe departs from psychological probability."[13] For Watt's *Rise of the Novel*, significantly, *Robinson Crusoe* is both designated as "the first novel" and also strangely tangential to Watt's core thesis, which counterposes Richardson and Fielding through Watt's important analysis of the relationship between "realism of presentation" and "realism of assessment."

Virginia Woolf helps us to explain this discrepancy and to define the tension within Watt's engagement with this novel. Woolf's account of *Robinson Crusoe* acknowledges the striking absence that Watt identified as a lack of "psychological probability":

> It is a masterpiece, and it is a masterpiece largely because Defoe . . . thwarts us and flouts us at every turn. . . . It is, we know, the story of a man who is thrown, after many perils and adventures, alone upon a desert island. The mere suggestion—peril and solitude and a desert island—is enough to rouse in us the expectation of some far land on the limits of the world; of the sun rising and the sun setting; of man, isolated from his kind, brooding alone upon the nature of society and the strange ways of men. Before we open the book we have perhaps vaguely sketched out the kind of pleasure we expect it to give us. We read; and we are rudely contradicted on every page. There are no sunsets and no sunrises; there is no solitude and no soul.[14]

But Woolf sees what Watt neglects: there is no human soul on *Robinson Crusoe*'s island, but there is a powerful nonhuman entity:

> There is no solitude and no soul. There is, on the contrary, staring us full in the face nothing but a large earthenware pot. . . . By believing fixedly in the solidity

---

12. Ian Watt, *The Rise of the Novel: Studies in Defoe, Richardson, and Fielding* (Berkeley: University of California Press, 1957), 72–74.

13. Watt, 88.

14. Virginia Woolf, from *The Second Common Reader* (1932), reprinted in *Robinson Crusoe: A Norton Critical Edition*, by Daniel Defoe, 2nd ed., ed. Michael Schinagel (New York: Norton, 1975), 285.

of the pot and its earthiness, [Defoe] has subdued every other element to his design. ... And is there any reason, we ask as we shut the book, why the perspective that a plain earthenware pot exacts should not satisfy us as completely, once we grasp it, as man himself in all his sublimity standing against a background of broken mountains and tumbling oceans with stars flaming in the sky?[15]

Woolf here registers the force of the material thing in this novel so strongly that she posits a dramatic contrast with "man himself"—with human subjectivity—in which even the most "sublime" definition of human being does not eclipse the power of the pot. In fact, as Woolf expresses the self-efficacy of the pot here, the thing actually gathers the sublimity of the world—as seen through human being—into its own solidity and completeness.[16]

Woolf's eloquence—or her ventriloquy of *Robinson Crusoe*'s eloquence on behalf of the pot—urges us to extrapolate across the scope of the robinsonade—whose purview extends from castaways to labor value and from homemaking to children's instruction—to posit a powerful counterhuman through line in the reception of *Robinson Crusoe* over the past three centuries: the "completeness" of the material thing even in the face of "man himself in all his sublimity." The pot is an intuitive icon for this completeness. In fact, this pot has become a very resonant metonymy, on its own, for the power of the thing independent of the human. Like Woolf, Bill Brown, in recounting Heidegger's conceptualization of the "thing" as a resource for new materialist thinking, also portrays this same powerful pot. Brown calls attention to Heidegger's notion of *das Krug*: its "independence," its "self-sameness," the "force of [its] form," its capacity to "be in its Being" and by that means ("thinging") to make the world manifest—"the thing things world."[17] This capacity of completeness is a kind of climax in the theorization of new materialism

---

15. Woolf, 285, 287.
16. Lydia H. Liu connects materialism and colonialism through Defoe's pot. She sees this moment of efficacy in Woolf's account as a "fetishized metonomy ... between man and the thing he makes," demonstrating that Defoe's pot is an unacknowledged product of the eighteenth-century "global network of the porcelain trade" and thus that Defoe's text is powerfully formative of the "colonial disavowal" that underlies eighteenth-century imaginative literature. Liu, "Robinson Crusoe's Earthenware Pot: Science, Aesthetics, and the Metaphysics of True Porcelain," in *Romantic Science: The Literary Forms of Natural History*, ed. Noah Heringman (Albany: State University of New York Press, 2003), 139, 146.
17. Bill Brown, *Other Things* (Chicago: University of Chicago Press, 2015), 29–30; Martin Heidegger, "The Thing," in *Poetry, Language, Thought*, trans. Martin Hofstader (New York: Harper and Row, 1971), 175, 178. Heidegger uses "thinging" here in the following context: "The

for Brown. He argues that it "culminates Heidegger's strategy for thinking beyond the Subject, . . . for overcoming the merely ontic and the
merely phenomenological: for overcoming the subject."[18]

And just as the encounter with the pot enables Woolf to assemble the scene
of "man himself" and his "mountains, . . . oceans, . . . and sky," *das Krug*
raises for Heidegger the status of the maker of the pot—or, in its originary
occasion, Crusoe the potter. The potter—even or especially Crusoe—serves
only to establish the solidity of the pot as an object of production: the completeness of the pot. Brown develops Heidegger's account of the potter's "giving way" to the pot by emphasizing the potter's solitude and by focusing on the
potter's definition as producer rather than consumer: "[Heidegger casts]
the potter as the sole human actor to emphasize the production of the object
rather than, say its consumption or its use. And once the potter exists, the
objectness of the object (its relation to a subject) can give way to the thingness of the thing. . . . Thingness here, . . . the (indissociable) thinging of the
world, names an activity, a productive function—but an activity animated
by no human aim."[19] This Heideggerian pot, Brown shows us, has a long-
standing heritage. *Das Krug* comes to Heidegger by way of Georg Simmel,
Ernst Bloch, and Theodore Adorno—from Simmel's engagement with the
handle of *das Krug* as a mediating instrument for negotiating the subject-
object relation to Bloch's understanding of *das Krug* as "the imbrication of
subject and object" to Adorno's offering that "the hollow depths of the pot
express . . . not a metaphor; to be in those depths . . . would be to be in the
thing-in-itself, in what it is in the nature of the human being that eludes in-
trospection." And, as Brown then argues, "in Heidegger's rewriting of the
episode, such concern for the human being . . . is effectively beside the point,
except insofar as they are assembled (gathered) by the thing."[20]

These counterhuman anecdotes of a jar—its completeness, its self-
efficacy, its power of "thinging," its "dominion everywhere"—suggest
that the pot is a heuristic for modernity's engagement with and theoriza-

jug is a thing insofar as it things. The presence of something present such as the jug comes into its
own, appropriatively manifests and determines itself, only from the thinging of the thing."

18. Brown, *Other Things*, 30.

19. Brown, 31.

20. Theodore Adorno, "The Handle, the Pot, and Early Experience," in *Notes to Literature*,
vol. 2, ed. Rolf Tiedeman, trans. Shierry Weber Nicholson (New York: Columbia University
Press, 1992), 218; Brown, *Other Things*, 31.

tion of materialism.[21] In this sense, Heidegger, Bloch, and Adorno's pot enables us to see the prescience of Woolf's understanding of Defoe's pot, going forward in this history. Or, going backward, Woolf's pot marks the ongoing realization of Defoe's iconic materialist vision, now redacted as a (so-called) "new" materialism. All these portrayals of the pot implement *Robinson Crusoe*'s counterhuman redefinition of matter, of the complete "thing" as possessed of a new force "standing against" the "sublimity" of the human.

II

Newton's understanding of gravity launched a vigorous, visible, sustained debate about whether the forces of repulsion and attraction—the motion observed in particles affected by gravitation—were an indication of powers inherent in matter itself or were imposed by an external source. According to John W. Yolton, "the understanding of gravitation and motion centered on what matter was thought to be capable of on its own."[22] This question of matter's power or completeness "on its own" was a nexus of tension in Newtonian thought and in the scientific, philosophical, and theological debates of the eighteenth century. In this context, as Ernan McMullin asserts, "Newton was trying to reshape the entire conception of matter" for the new science and for modern ontology, in an effort that was an ongoing process of

21. Wallace Stevens, "Anecdote of the Jar" (1919), *The Collected Poems of Wallace Stevens* (Knopf: New York, 1954), 76.

> I placed a jar in Tennessee,
> And round it was, upon a hill.
> It made the slovenly wilderness
> Surround that hill.
>
> The wilderness rose up to it,
> And sprawled around, no longer wild.
> The jar was round upon the ground
> And tall and of a port in air.
>
> It took dominion everywhere.
> The jar was gray and bare.
> It did not give of bird or bush,
> Like nothing else in Tennessee.

22. John W. Yolton, *Thinking Matter: Materialism in Eighteenth-Century Britain* (Minneapolis: University of Minnesota Press, 1984), 94.

reflection and revision. McMullin shows that Newton's laws of motion and their corollaries, examined in context, while clearly indicating "the abandonment of the principle of the strict passivity of matter which had so heavily influenced earlier mechanics, . . . [reflect] obvious ambiguity, [which] was to give Newtonians many a headache in the century that followed." This ambiguity arose from Newton's simultaneous insistence both on the existence of "force" and on the inertness of matter, through his representation of inertia—the *vis inertiae*—as itself a *vis insita*—a form of "force." McMullin explains that "in the story of the concept of matter, Newton plays a paradoxical role. . . . He struggled with the intricacies of this concept for sixty years while building his system of the world around it. Yet . . . he provided scientists with a neat and manageable substitute for it, one which would later supplant the older concept in the explicit symbolic systems of modern science."[23]

In Newton's representations of the capacity of matter, throughout his works, the operative and challenging words were "force," "power," "energy," "pulling," "attraction," and "acting upon." Though Newton often sought to weaken this portrayal of active or vital forces by claiming that his language was figurative or that these notions were only mathematical, his readers interpreted these words to indicate that "gravitational force existed truly" and that they constituted, as Robert E. Schofield argues, "a new dynamic theory of matter."[24] McMullin describes the ways in which Newton in the *Principia* attempted to "restrict that work to an ontologically neutral sense of such dynamic terms, . . . a sense which would be descriptive and mathematical, merely attributing certain sorts of regularity of motion to one body in proximity to another, without postulating the kind of agency responsible. . . . [But] Newton's terminology was difficult to de-ontologize in this way. When he spoke . . . of bodies 'attracting,' or 'pulling,' or 'acting upon' one another, it was difficult to take these words as figures of speech. . . . Not only were his critics unpersuaded, but Newton, in his incessant drafting and redrafting, was just as prone as they to take such terms as 'attraction' to mean what they say."[25]

23. McMullin, *Newton on Matter and Energy*, 1, 35, 1.

24. Robert E. Schofield, *Mechanism and Materialism: British Natural Philosophy in an Age of Reason* (Princeton, NJ: Princeton University Press, 1970), 8–9. Also see McMullin, *Newton on Matter and Energy*, 144n135, for examples of Newton's attempts to "de-ontologize."

25. McMullin, *Newton on Matter and Energy*, 70–71.

Newton's most direct and sustained claim for the intrinsic motive force of matter occurs in the second edition of the *Optics* (1713), to which he added a set of "Queries" that "gave Newton greater freedom to speak more openly."[26] Query 31 states,

> Have not the small Particles of Bodies certain Powers, Virtues or Forces, by which they act at a distance, not only upon the Rays of Light for reflecting, refracting, and inflecting them, but also upon one another for producing a great Part of the Phænomena of nature? For it's well known that Bodies act one upon another by the Attractions of Gravity, Magnetism, and Electricity; and these Instances show the Tenor and Course of Nature, and make it not improbable but that there may be more attractive Powers than these.[27]

Newton's portrayal of these "powers" may be attributable to his study of alchemy. In describing Newton's alchemical notes from the decades from 1675 to 1695, McMullin shows that he was

> seeking clues to the nature of chemical and vital processes and because the mechanical philosophy could not help him, alchemy seemed a likely place to look. . . . The alchemical literature he pored over was full of references to the active principles responsible for the transformations of matter. The alchemists' belief was that the matter of all things is one and the same, and that variety and activity alike come from the animating principles they disguised under code names. . . . The gradual transition from alchemy to chemistry in no way diminished Newton's conviction that the world is permeated by active principles of all kinds.[28]

The recent recognition of Newton's references to alchemy highlights our appreciation of the significance and scope of his redefinition of matter, for the realms both of knowledge and of the imagination.

The notion of the inherent capacity or completeness of matter is a motivating component of contemporary thought, extending from Newton across

---

26. Yolton, *Thinking Matter*, 93.

27. Isaac Newton, *Optics*, based on the 4th ed. (London, 1730; repr., Mineola, NY: Dover, 1952), Query 31, p. 376.

28. McMullin, *Newton on Matter and Energy*, 41–45.

philosophical and theological discourse. For Locke, the question of the power of matter "on its own" is construed in terms of the power of "thinking":

> We have the ideas of *matter* and *thinking*, but possibly shall never be able to know, whether any mere material being thinks, or no; it being impossible for us, by the contemplation of our own ideas, without revelation, to discover, whether Omnipotency has not given to some systems of matter fitly disposed, a power to perceive and think, or else joined and fixed to matter so disposed, a thinking immaterial substance. . . . For since we must allow he has annexed effects to motion, which we can no way conceive motion able to produce, what reason have we to conclude, that he could not order them as well to be produced in a subject we cannot conceive capable of them, as well as in a subject we cannot conceive the motion of matter can any way operate upon?[29]

The proposal, for Locke, is expressed as a core ontological challenge—in Yolton's words, "could thought be an intrinsic or natural property of matter?"[30] And Locke explicitly expressed the corollary assertion that the immortal spirit need not be linked exclusively to immateriality:

> The properties of a rose, a peach, or an elephant, superadded to matter, change not the properties of matter; but matter is in these things matter still. But if one venture to go on one step further, and say, God may give to matter thought, reason, and volition, as well as sense and spontaneous motion, there are men ready presently to . . . tell us that he cannot do it; because it destroys the essence. . . . But whatever excellency, not contained in its essence, be superadded to matter, it does not destroy the essence of matter, if it leaves it an extended solid substance; wherever that is, there is the essence of matter.[31]

The objection that Locke cites here reflects the urgent contemporary negotiation around the capacity of bodies in themselves: whether bodies are essentially, intrinsically defined by inherent activity or whether power, force, or "thought" is not attributable to bodies themselves but rather arises from an

---

29. John Locke, *An Essay Concerning Human Understanding*, abr. ed., ed. Kenneth P. Winkler (Indianapolis: Hackett, 1996), 4.3.6, pp. 236–37.

30. Yolton, *Thinking Matter*, 92.

31. Locke, *Essay Concerning Human Understanding*, "Stillingfleet Correspondence," 349; cited in Yolton, *Thinking Matter*, 18.

external source. The translation from the material to the theological debate was immediate for Locke, Newton, and their contemporaries. And the counterposition to the activity of matter—the notion that matter is "inactive, impenetrable, and resistant to change [and] has no active powers"—is expressed as the argument that "all those effects currently ascribed to certain natural [or inherent] powers residing in matter are immediately produced by the power of an immaterial Being.'"[32] In Yolton's account of this debate, he demonstrates the scope and impact of this issue, for Andrew Baxter, Joseph Priestley, George Berkeley, George Cheyne, Samuel Clarke, Robert Clayton, Anthony Collins, David Hartley, David Hume, Isaac Watts, and Richard Price, among others, showing that this challenge "raised a storm of protest and discussion right through to the last years of the eighteenth century."[33]

The Newtonian representation of matter is significant methodologically as well as conceptually. Throughout Newton's lifelong engagement with the material world, he sought to model a form of knowledge-creation and a mode of discourse that emerge directly from experience. Method, of course, is fundamental to Newton's contribution to the establishment of experimental philosophy, and Newton explicitly promoted and systematically pursued experiential reasoning in all his work. McMullin shows how, in the case of any particular physical claim or theory, Newton persistently seeks to argue from "an experienced property of experienced bodies"; for Newton, this experiential stance is a direct methodological counter to the "rational reflection so much relied on by Descartes."[34] Newton expresses his commitment to this method directly in Query 31 (*Optics*): "to derive two or three general Principles of Motion from Phænomena, and afterwards to tell us how the Properties and Actions of all corporal Things follow from these manifest Principles, would be a very great step in Philosophy, though the Causes of those Principles were not yet discover'd."[35] Query 8 (*Optics*) illustrates the experimental method and compellingly highlights its rhetorical tenor and its distinctive discursive effect. Here Newton is describing the sources of vibrations that cause bodies to emit light:

---

32. Yolton, 96, 95, citing Andrew Baxter, *An Enquiry into the Nature of the Human Soul*, vol. 1, 2nd ed. (London, 1737), sec. 2 heading, p. 79.

33. Yolton, 17.

34. McMullin, *Newton on Matter and Energy*, 23.

35. Newton, *Optics*, 401–402.

As for instance; Sea-Water in a raging storm; Quick-silver agitated in *vacuo*; the Back of a Cat, or Neck of a Horse, obliquely struck or rubbed in a dark place; Wood, Flesh and Fish while they putrefy; Vapours arising from putrefy'd Waters, usually call'd *Ignis Fatui*; Stacks of moist Hay or Corn growing hot by fermentation; Glow-worms and the Eyes of some Animals by vital Motions; the vulgar *Phosphorus* agitated by the attrition of any Body, or by the acid Particles of the Air; Amber and some Diamonds by striking, pressing or rubbing them; Scrapings of Steel struck off by a Flint; Iron hammer'd very nimbly till it become so hot as to kindle Sulphur thrown upon it; the Axletrees of Chariots taking fire by the rapid rotation of the Wheels.[36]

Here, the wood, the hay or corn, the scrapings of steel, the amber and diamonds, the axletrees of chariots—these are Newton's "things," powerful in their efficacy, their solidity, and their completeness as "experienced bodies."

Newton's formidable contribution to the contemporary engagement with matter and experienced things matches up with *Robinson Crusoe*'s imaginative world, in a way that suggests a connection between literature and experimental philosophy at the moment when materialism finds its modern formulation. This connection suggests, first, that natural history's theory of matter and *Robinson Crusoe*'s portrayal of things are, both, both conceptual and methodological, in the sense that they engage the representation or experience of objects, in order to offer a new way of understanding the essence of the material world. Second, if Defoe's things are placed in the Newtonian context, they offer a distinctive perspective on the material and narrative premises and the discursive traits of modern realism.

III

Robinson Crusoe is an experiment in the representation of force. The novel is full of energy and activity: the solidity and completeness of Crusoe's pot is framed by a set of shifting, intense, and vibrant scenes of action for its own

36. Newton, 340–41. Milton Wilson cites this passage in his account of "literary invention" in Newton: "Reading Locke and Newton as Literature," *University of Toronto Quarterly* 57 (1988): 477–78.

sake. These are unmoored, contingent scenarios of indiscriminate force. They express an unbounded, "rough and terrible" energy, but they are conceptually rationalized by reference to contemporary religious and economic institutions—from Protestantism and from financial models of risk and speculation.[37] First, referencing a prominent strain of Protestant ethics, the novel describes Crusoe's emphatic rejection of his father's counsel to "settle" for the "easy circumstances" of the "middle Station of Life" (Defoe, 5, 6). The subsequent scenes of action and adventure enable Crusoe, in embracing contingency, to demonstrate the Protestant principle of submission to divine providence: Martin Luther describes the true Christian as "not presuming upon the future, and not trusting in any man or in oneself but clinging to God alone."[38] Thus Crusoe—and the text itself—pursues activity, "adventures," and "undertakings out of the common road" (Defoe, 4–6). In this context, uncertainty in regard to the engagement in the turbulent affairs of that world becomes an end in itself, and the allusion to doctrinal principle is matched by an immediate release of narrative energy.

Second, the context of unpredictable economic activity and risk, which is reflected in Crusoe's choice of "enterprize" over "the middle State" (Defoe, 5), evokes the core tenet of venture capitalism, with its direct activation of contingency and indeterminacy as sine qua non. The vital economic engagement with risk—the accelerating speculation of the stock exchange; the institutionalization of risk in the rise of international capital markets, loans and mortgages, credit and debt, discounts, shares, futures, and securities; the attempts to manage risk in the establishment of actuarial science and in the development of joint stock charters and insurance—all attest to the centrality of contingent activity to the so-called financial revolution of the eighteenth century. Here, indeterminacy underwrites "a highly speculative and volatile economy, full of enterprise and initiative, open to an extraordinary degree to the vagaries of fashion and fad, encouraging quick returns and setting a premium on highly flexible and imaginative business strategies"—the

37. Daniel Defoe, *Robinson Crusoe: A Norton Critical Edition*, ed. Michael Shinagel (New York: Norton, 1994), 8. Subsequent references to this source appear parenthetically in the text.
38. Martin Luther, *Trade and Usury*, in *Luther's Works*, vol. 45, ed. Walther I. Brandt and Helmut T. Lehman (Minneapolis: Fortress, 1962), 257. For this argument, see Dwight Codr, *Raving at Usurers: Anti-finance and the Ethics of Uncertainty in England, 1690–1750* (Charlottesville: University of Virginia Press, 2016).

"Ambition," "Vicissitudes," "Uneasinesses," and volatile activity that Crusoe's father describes in his warnings to his son (Defoe, 5).[39]

The opening scenes of *Robinson Crusoe* dramatically and repeatedly enact these imaginative engagements with energy and force. The sequence of storm scenes that take control of the narrative upon Crusoe's leaving his father's house introduce and immediately highlight this representation of unmoored, dynamic activity. The portrayal of the ocean reflects an immense, unfocused, and shifting counterhuman power:

> The Sea went Mountains high, and broke upon us every three or four Minutes: when I could look about, I could see nothing but Distress round us: Two Ships that rid near us we found had cut their Masts by the Board, being deep loaden; and our Men cry'd out, that a Ship which rid about a Mile a-Head of us was foundered. Two more Ships being driven from their Anchors, were run out of the Roads to Sea at all Adventures, and that with not a Mast standing. The light Ships fared the best, as not so much laboring in the Sea; but two or three of them drove, and came close by us, running away with only their Sprit-sail out before the Wind. (10)

Formally, this account is multifaceted, proliferative, and directionless: it refers to size ("Mountains high"), to speed ("running away ... before the Wind"), and to dispersed action ("near us," "a Mile a-Head of us," "out of the Roads to Sea," "close by us") all at once. To "look about" in this world is to step out of an artificial assertion of "Temperance, Moderation, Quietness" into the experience of unstructured power and force.

This experiment with the representation of force dominates the pre-island imaginative experience of *Robinson Crusoe*, generating a persistent sense of proximate vitality: more storms, more "Mountain-like" waves of "mighty Force," a fight with pirates, and even an encounter with a "dreadful Monster" (22). And all this energy results in more decisions "hurried on" or "push'd ... forward" in a scenario characterized by ongoing "Confusion of Thought" (31, 12, 34).

The island systematically and suddenly redirects this vitality and resolves this confusion. Storms, waves, winds, pirates, and monsters are decisively re-

---

39. John Brewer, "Commercialization and Politics," in *The Birth of a Consumer Society: The Commercialization of Eighteenth-Century England*, ed. Neil McKendrick, Brewer, and J. H. Plumb (Bloomington: Indiana University Press, 1982), 213.

placed by a sequential proliferation of objects. The narrative retains the rapidity generated by the storms, as well as the attitude of experimental succession portrayed in those rapidly repeated opening scenes, but turns now to a focused imaginative engagement with materiality itself. The "desert island" is a singular enabling locale for this experiment with matter because it excludes the multifaceted vortices of energy that fill the world beyond its perimeter. Its isolation and barrenness offer a focal point for force and turn that focus to the narrative engagement with objects—with "experienced bodies"— whose powerful collective self-efficacy, like that of Newton's list of the sources of vibrations in bodies, is revealed through the experimental method that assembles them.

This engagement with the material world is marked by an impersonal momentum, which repeatedly gathers a "strange multitude of little Things" (86) into a generative sequence of production—a sequence that impels the objects into motion and change in relation to each other. One "Thing" gives rise to another "Thing," in a series that occupies the attention of the reader and the producer (Crusoe) and that populates the island world itself—in an activity that is aligned with Heidegger's "thinging" and that expresses the systematic self-containment of the counterhuman. Here is the sequence of production of the earthenware pot, beginning with "the Clay":

> [I must] dig it [the Clay], . . . temper it, . . . bring it home and work it; . . . [then make] two large earthen ugly things, . . . Jarrs, ... [which lead next to] little round Pots, flat Dishes, Pitchers, and Pipkins, [then comes the firing of the pots]. . . . I . . . plac'd three large Pipkins, and two or three Pots in a Pile one upon another, and plac'd my fire-wood all around it with a great Heap of Embers under them; I ply'd the Fire with fresh Fuel round the out-side, and upon the top, till I saw the Pots in the inside red hot quite thro', and observ'd that they did not crack at all; when I saw them clear red, I let them stand in that Heat about 5 or 6 Hours, till I found one of them, tho'd it did not crack, did melt or run, . . . so I slack'd my Fire gradually till the Pots began to abate of the red Colour, and . . . in the Morning I had three very good, I will not say handsome Pipkins; and two other Earthen Pots, as hard burnt as cou'd be desir'd; and one of them perfectly glaz'd with the Running of the Sand. (88–89)

"Clay" brings forth "Jarrs"; next come a proliferation of "little round Pots, flat Dishes, Pitchers and Pipkins," which then become the glazed "Earthen

Pots." Those then lead to the generation of the "Mortar," the "Pestle," and the "Sieve":

> I had made an Earthen Pot that would bear the Fire. . . . My next Concern was, to get me a Stone Mortar, to stamp or beat some Corn in. . . . After a great deal of Time lost in searching for a Stone I gave it over, and resolv'd to look out for a great Block of hard Wood, . . . and getting one as big as I had Strength to stir, I rounded it, and form'd it in the Out-side with my Axe and hatchet, and then with the Help of Fire, and infinite Labour, made a hollow Place in it. . . . After this, I made a great heavy Pestle or Beater, of the Wood call'd the Iron-wood. . . . My next Difficulty was to make a Sieve, or Search, to dress my Meal, and to part it from the Bran. . . . At last I did remember I had among the Seamens Cloths which were sav'd out of the Ship, some Neckcloths of Callicoe, or Muslin; and with some Pieces of these, I made three small Sieves. (88–89)

Activity is incessant in these sequences. Locally, the energy is portrayed through an allusion to the local contributions of the producer—"I ply'd the fire," "as I had Strength to Stir"—but in the broader structure of these passages, energy is generated by the rapid, sequential emergence of the things, one after another. This energy is absorbed into the things that are represented as its outcome—in the sense that these things themselves, in their hurried transformation to a subsequent product, reflect a restlessness and potential for changeableness.

Again, here the following account of the progress of production of a "long Shelf" describes an irresistible trajectory marked by an engagement with "inexpressible" energy:

> A large Tree . . . was to be cut down, because my Board was to be a broad one. This Tree I was three Days a cutting down, and two more cutting off the Bows, and reducing it to a Log, or Piece of Timber. With inexpressible hacking and hewing I reduc'd both Sides of it into Chips, till it begun to be light enough to move; then I turn'd it, and made one Side of it smooth, and flat, as a Board from End to End; then turning that Side downward, cut the other Side, till I brought the Plank to be about three Inches thick, and smooth on both sides. (84)

In the course of the movement from a "large Tree" to a "Log, or Piece of Timber" to a "Board" to a "Plank" and to a "long Shelf," the producer's "hacking and hewing" is another local signal—pointing to the force empowering the cumulative generation of objects in the sequence.

The experiment in the representation of force, on *Robinson Crusoe*'s island, takes the form of rapid and irresistible sequence. The successive presence of these things generates a narrative energy and attaches a portrayal of vitality to matter itself. As we have seen here, Crusoe's plying, cutting, hacking, hewing, and stirring is systematically absorbed into the activity of the things so as to augment their own material force. This counterhuman force is an immediate narrative effect of these passages, and it highlights these things themselves as a vital presence—for Crusoe and for the reader. Crusoe's solitary, repetitive, incessant activity enables the irresistible trajectory of the things themselves to dominate the narrative, foregrounding the "thingness" of these things and their consequent power of "thinging." As Heidegger argues, the potter's solitude demonstrates the thing-oriented activity of production rather than the human-oriented phenomenon of consumption, leaving the thing as "an activity animated by no human aim."[40] In Heidegger's concept, "That which in the jug's nature is its own is never brought about by its making. Now released from the making process, the self-supporting jug has to gather itself for the task of containing. In the process of its making . . . the jug must first show its outward appearance to the maker. But what shows itself here . . . characterizes the jug solely in the respect in which the vessel stands over against the maker as something to be made."[41] Lynn Festa, from her focus on the discursive function of objects in relation to novelistic subjectivity, turns this "thinging" process toward the potter himself: "What we are given to see of the object—what Crusoe's narrative describes—constitutes much of what we get of Crusoe's subjectivity. . . . Character emerges through the subjective perception of objects, rather than through the transparent depiction of inwardness."[42]

Through this distinctive narrative impact, then, the force of the succession of "Things" constitutes a materialist premise, a theory of "Thinging." Before the assemblage of "Things," the island is emphatically "barren" (Defoe, 40). Crusoe's first awareness, when he "began to look round" to "see what kind of Place" he was in, results in the observation, "in a Word, I had

---

40. Brown, *Other Things*, 31.
41. Heidegger, "Thing," 166.
42. Festa, 452.

nothing" (35–36). And this context of "nothing" immediately sets off a fre-
netic sequence in the assembly of Things from the grounded ship: "Bisket,"
"Rum," "Cordial Waters," "two Pistols," "rusty Swords," "Barrels of Pow-
der," "two Saws, an Axe, and a Hammer" (37–38), and then:

> I now began to consider, that I might yet get a great many Things out of the
> Ship. . . . I resolv'd to set all other Things apart, 'till I got every Thing out of
> the Ship that I could get. . . . I brought away several Things very useful to
> me. . . . Bags full of Nails and Spikes, a great Skrew-Jack, a Dozen or two of
> Hatchets, and . . . that most useful Thing call'd a Grindstone. . . . Besides
> these Things, I took all the Mens Cloaths that I could find, and a spare Fore-
> top-sail, a Hammock, and some bedding. (40–41)

As a site of isolation and barrenness, the island immediately prompts the
gathering of "Things": in fact, the island is entirely constituted by these in-
coming "Things." The "Earthen Pot" is a condensed example of this narrative's focused engagement with the vitality of matter; it stands for the array
of "Things" that populate *Robinson Crusoe*'s "desert island"—"thinging" its
central site of absence, making it manifest as a world.

IV

This encounter—between the "inexpressible" energy of *Robinson Crusoe*'s
things and Newton's experiments with force—reflects the scope and impact of
the modern engagement with matter. It records the mutually constitutive roles
of imaginative literature and the new science for modern materialism. Tita
Chico makes this mutuality the premise of her study of "the experimental
imagination": Chico seeks to define "the historical moment when what we
now think of as literature and science were not codified as distinct epistemolo-
gies, but were understood as deeply . . . implicated in one another . . . [to] reveal
a doubled epistemological trajectory: experimental observation utilizes imaginative speculation and imaginative fancy enables new forms of understanding."[43]

The encounter between *Robinson Crusoe* and Newton, in a "doubled epistemological trajectory," brings two manifestations of materialism into view,

---

43. Tita Chico, *The Experimental Imagination: Literary Knowledge and Science in the British
Enlightenment* (Stanford, CA: Stanford University Press, 2020), 3.

both for the eighteenth century and for our own time. First, the perspective provided by Newton demonstrates the manner by which and the particular components in terms of which modern matter is founded—in an inductive, conjectural process that records the tangible world of Newtonian physics. Today's "new" materialism emerges from that process and that world; viewing its conceptualization through the lens of Newton, then, explains and specifies current claims for the vitality and power, for the self-efficacy and autonomy, and for the movement of material things. In this context, for instance, Jane Bennett's eloquent effort to "theorize a vitality intrinsic to materiality as such, and to detach materiality from the figures of passive, mechanistic, or divinely infused substance" can be understood as an acknowledgment of a powerful modern hermeneutic, rather than an "estrangement."[44]

Second, the perspective provided by *Robinson Crusoe* suggests that that very inductive process—driven by the representation of "experienced bodies" and leading on sequentially from body to body or from thing to thing—is activated through the literary imagination as a narrative of irresistible succession. This is the literary form of modern matter; things acquire their force, exhibit their vitality, and make the world of the island manifest through this discursive enactment of counterhuman vitality. *Robinson Crusoe*, then, offers a formal model for the mobilization of matter for literary critique and for the counterhuman imaginary, within a particular text and in literary history. This model brings to earth the wide range of outcomes that has been assigned by new materialist critique to the portrayal of "things"—from power or autonomy to disruption or obstinate solitude to self-efficacy, expansiveness, or innovation. From this perspective, power, disruption, or innovation are all heuristics for the imaginative creation of gravitational force by means of the formal strategies of the counterhuman imaginary—a common ground that offers a basis for interpretive coherence for new materialist literary critique.

The modern engagement with matter through the activities of the counterhuman imaginary that we are here witnessing in Newton's "Queries" and *Robinson Crusoe* is an encompassing event, with vast consequences for modern thought and modern culture. Of course it shapes the science of physics, and it models empirical scientific method. It undergirds and continues to inform the modern conceptualization of economic forces. It establishes the

---

44. Bennett, *Vibrant Matter*, xiii.

discursive practice out of which the literary mode that we now call "realism" emerges—featuring the concrete, particular materials and experiences of a tangible, secular world. In describing the encompassing nature of this event across realms of understanding and imagination, Michael H. Turk includes the contributions of Montesquieu, Voltaire, Diderot, Adam Smith, and d'Alembert with those of Newton and Defoe in order to outline

> the bridging [of] the scientific with the philosophical and the literary. . . . One might take the general resemblance in . . . ideas [across these realms as] evidence of a commonality in consciousness, a mark of the intellectual currents, broadly understood, sweeping across Western Europe in the course of the eighteenth century. Those established an environment in which the conjectural, imagined as such or even cast in the form of fiction, would be perceived as leading to the construction or expansion of defined fields of knowledge.[45]

The pot is both a form of knowledge and a form of imagination: as knowledge, it records the inductive character of modern matter; as a founding facet of the counterhuman imaginary, it asserts the vitality of the other-than-human world, even while it is experienced through human creativity.

---

45. Michael H. Turk, "Economics as Plausible Conjecture," *History of Political Economy* 42 (2010): 533–34.

Plate XIX.

Vol. V. facing y̆ Title

Here strip my Children here at once leap in
Here prove who best can dash thro' thick & thin.

Dunciad Book II.

Figure 3. *Fleet River* (ca. 1750), by Francis Hayman.
Image © London Metropolitan Archives (City of London).

Chapter 3

THE UNCREATION OF THE HUMAN

Pope's Dunciad

Alexander Pope's *Dunciad* (1728, 1743) is among literary history's sustained and direct imaginative engagements with human creativity. Mocking the epic battles and mythological scenarios of Virgil and Homer, *The Dunciad* attacks— by "praising"—a wide and ultimately identifiable number of writers in Pope's contemporary London, especially highlighting in the final four-book version of the poem the playwright Colley Cibber as the new King of Dunces. In effect, *The Dunciad* is a directory of the literary efforts and writers of the day, and the scope of its frame of reference testifies to its obsessive attention to human creativity: Edmund Curll, Bernard Lintot, Jacob Tonson, John Dennis, Ambrose Philips, Nahum Tate, Daniel Defoe, Elkanah Settle, Lewis Theobald, James Ralph, George Ridpath, Abel Roper, Nathaniel Mist, Thomas Shadwell, Elizabeth Thomas, Thomas Cook, Matthew Concanen, John Tutchin, Edward Ward, John Ozell, James Moore Smythe, Eliza Haywood, Thomas Osborne, Leonard Welsted, John Breval, Besaleel Morris, William Bond, William Webster, Thomas Blackmore, John Oldmixon, Edward Roome, William Arnall, Benjamin Norton Defoe,

Jonathan Smedley, James Pitt, Susanna Centlivre, Bernard Mandeville, William Mears, Thomas Warner, William Wilkins, Thomas Durfey, Giles Jacob, William Popple, Philip Horneck, Edward Roome, Barnham Goode, Charles Gildon, Thomas Burnet, George Duckett, Thomas Hanmer, William Benson, Richard Bentley, and Joseph Wasse.[1] And well beyond its own historical moment, the poem also reflects in detail on the human engagement with the arts across the ages of the western European canon, including Cervantes, Rabelais, Swift, Fletcher, Molière, Shakespeare, Corneille, Congreve, Addison, Prior, Bacon, Newton, Locke, and Milton.

But in this context of human creativity, strikingly and unexpectedly, *The Dunciad* is also pervasively engaged with the other-than-human—its powers, its agency, and its processes of assemblage, interaction, and turbulence. Tracking those manifestations of the other-than-human in *The Dunciad* engages and extends the analytical practice that recent new materialist critics have developed from new work in the physical and the life sciences.[2] Quantum physics has inspired concepts around agency and interrelationality that have been taken up by new materialist theorists and that are directly relevant to *The Dunciad*. Karen Barad, in *Meeting the Universe Half Way: Quantum Physics and the Entanglement of Matter and Meaning*, offers an influential conceptualization for the inherent force of matter, which she terms "agential realism." Barad uses modern physics as a model for a rejection of traditional subject/object rationales in favor of "intra-action":

> The neologism "intra-action" *signifies the mutual constitution of entangled agencies*. A lively new ontology emerges: the world's radical aliveness comes to light in an entirely nontraditional way that reworks the nature of both relationality and aliveness (vitality, dynamism, agency). This shift in ontology also entails a reconceptualization of other core philosophical concepts such as space, time, matter, dynamics, agency, structure, subjectivity, objectivity,

---

1. See Laura Brown, *Fables of Modernity: Literature and Culture in the English Eighteenth Century* (Ithaca, NY: Cornell University Press, 2001), 136.

2. "Unprecedented things are currently being done with and to matter, nature, life, production, and reproduction," as Diana Coole and Samantha Frost have asserted, and those moves inspire new terms of engagement with matter, for literary studies. Coole and Frost, "Introducing the New Materialisms," in *New Materialisms: Ontology, Agency, and Politics*, ed. Coole and Frost (Durham, NC: Duke University Press, 2010), 4.

knowing, intentionality, discursivity, performativity, entanglement, and ethical engagement.[3]

We will shortly see the relevance of this reconceptualization of relationality to *The Dunciad*'s experiment with processes that run counter to human conventions of vertical or linear order.

Meanwhile Nikolas S. Rose, in his study of biomedicine, highlights the impact of new perspectives in molecular biology on thinking about culture. Rose describes the replacement of earlier biological notions of "depth" and of the corporeal "self" with a new scenario of "open circuits" that produce a "flattening" effect across a range of basic life processes. The result is a set of concepts that reflect an "emphasis on complexities, interactions, developmental sequences, and cascades of regulation interacting back and forth at various points in the metabolic pathways."[4] And Jane Bennett's *Vibrant Matter* couples these flattening, cascading, and interactional scenarios from the physical and the life sciences—along with corollary notions of interconnectivity from ecological and environmental philosophy—with a reengagement with the long tradition of vitalism or, as she terms it, "vital materialism" or "thing power." Bennett's attention to the "efficacy of objects in excess of the human meanings, designs, or purposes they express or serve" and her corollary focus on "vitality" invoke an ongoing anti-Cartesian tradition, whose eloquence, as she demonstrates, stretches from Lucretian and Spinozan vitalism to the current "Continental vitalism" of Henri Bergson, Gilles Deleuze, and Bruno Latour.[5]

Even more useful in an understanding of the counterhuman imaginary that emerges in *The Dunciad*, surprisingly, is the powerfully insightful perspective that Michel Serres's account of Lucretian atomism in *The Birth of Physics* has brought to recent thinking in both physics and philosophy. Serres has been persuasive in demonstrating the relevance of ancient atomism's theories of "discontinuity, multiplicity and contingency" to modern scientific

---

3. Karen Barad, *Meeting the Universe Halfway: Quantum Physics and the Entanglement of Matter and Meaning* (Durham, NC: Duke University Press, 2007), 33.

4. Nikolas S. Rose, *The Politics of Life Itself: Biomedicine, Power, and Subjectivity in the Twenty-First Century* (Princeton, NJ: Princeton University Press, 2007), 47.

5. Jane Bennett, *Vibrant Matter: A Political Ecology of Things* (Durham, NC: Duke University Press, 2010), 20.

and philosophical thought, which—through developments in quantum mechanics, thermodynamics, entropy, and chaos theory—are also deeply "informed by contingency, non-linearity, complexity, emergence and flow." David Webb and William Ross, who have made Serres's work accessible to a wide audience in and beyond the physical sciences, describe the relevance of Lucretius's atomism to modern thought: "It is here in the elements of uncertainty and openness characteristic of such theories [of thermodynamics, statistical mechanics, quantum theory, and nonlinear dynamics], that ancient atomism reasserts itself in modern physics. . . . The world to which it bears witness, the world described by Lucretius, is a place of turbulent flows, of chaos and the emergence of order by what classical metaphysics has taught us to call chance, but what ancient atomism also knew as necessity." Webb and Ross offer a compact summary of Serres's account of the "turbulence" of this world:

There is, therefore, no universal history, no unilinear development and therefore no single frame of reference within which all events may be encompassed. There cannot even be a reliable rule of translation by which one can navigate from one frame or region to another, or between the local and the global. There are multiple orders or rhythms of time, and events do not unfold uniformly. Indeed, time itself is described by Serres as the "fluctuation of turbulences" (BP XXX: 115) that open the dimension of time as a pocket, or pockets, of local and short-lived order within the laminar flow. The void, too, makes an important contribution to the aleatory character of Lucretian physics, serving to embed discontinuity in the first principles of atomism. As a consequence, no law can be universal and local conditions cannot be treated simply as particular instance of a universal order.[6]

The Dunciad offers powerful poetic versions of "turbulence," "flow," and "discontinuity," as we will see. It opens up a "void" and displays an ultimate "chaos," all projected contrapuntally through forms of the counterhuman imaginary, even despite the poem's allegiance to human creativity.

Attention to these notions of vitality, dynamism, entanglement, assemblage, interrelation, flattening, chaos, fluidity, turbulence, or cascading in

6. David Webb and William Ross, introduction to *The Birth of Physics*, by Michel Serres, trans. Webb and Ross (Lanham, MD: Rowman and Littlefield, 2018), 2, 3–4, 6–7 (originally published 1977).

The Dunciad opens a formal route to an analysis of the counterhuman imaginary—a route that is grounded in the poem's local connections with Newton's theory of gravitation. *The Dunciad* pursues the same engagement with contemporary Newtonian notions of gravitational force that we can discover in Defoe's *Robinson Crusoe*. We know from other works in Pope's corpus that Pope was attentive to the current debates around Newton's theories. In *The Essay on Man* (1733–34), Newton is explicitly named and celebrated by Pope as the "mortal man [who] unfold[s] all Nature's law."[7] And Elizabeth Kowaleski Wallace in her essay on *The Rape of the Lock* (1714) has demonstrated Pope's awareness of current debates "concerning the nature of the physical universe and the material world, as well as the very principles by which it moves and transforms itself—in other words, the very extent to which the physical world might possess (despite indications to the contrary) excess, force, and vitality."[8]

The Dunciad refers only briefly to Newton directly by name, but the "law" of gravitation and the language that Newton used to describe the force of gravity are pervasive throughout the poem.[9] William Kinsley in his study of "physico-demonology in Pope's *Dunciad*" has demonstrated the prevalence of "Newtonian concepts and terms . . . [such that] we can find duncical counterparts for all the Newtonian analogies."[10] The references to and even dependence on gravitational force in Pope's poem are so extensive that *The Dunciad* could be understood as the literary enactment Newtonian physics. The poem details the "reshap[ing] of the entire conception of matter" that Ernan McMullin has described as the contemporary impact of Newtonian physics—a "reshaping" that involves a replacement of "the principle of the strict passivity of matter" with the observation of a force inherent in matter

---

7. Alexander Pope, *An Essay on Man*, in *Poetry and Prose of Alexander Pope*, ed. Aubrey Williams (Boston: Houghton Mifflin, 1969), 2.32.

8. Elizabeth Kowaleski Wallace, "The Things Things Don't Say: *The Rape of the Lock*: Vitalism, and New Materialism," *The Eighteenth Century* 59 (2018): 114.

9. Alexander Pope, *The Dunciad in Four Books*, in *Poetry and Prose of Alexander Pope*, 3.215–16:

'Tis yours, a Bacon or a Locke to blame,
A Newton's genius, or a Milton's flame:
But oh! with One, immortal one dispense,
The source of Newton's Light, of Bacon's Sense!

Subsequent references to this source are cited parenthetically in the text.

10. William Kinsley, "Physico-demonology in Pope's *Dunciad*," *Modern Language Review* 70 (1975): 26.

itself.[11] As the "counterparts" in imaginative literature for "all the Newtonian analogies" that sought to express gravitation, *The Dunciad*'s poetic instantiations of gravitation offer a distinctive opportunity to apprehend the contemporary representation of the force inherent in matter from within a discursive realm separate from that of the new science. The poem invites us to ask how gravitation operates in the world of the human imagination.

I

The Dunciad is an extended poetical enactment of force, expressed as a pervasive "pow'r" flowing across and among a material world of "dunces," authors, publishers, books, lands, streams, oceans, and even suns and moons. The opening section of the last book of the poem offers a summary account of this power, which exercises a "Force inertly strong" (4.5–8). This passage summarizes the nature of the energy and the extent of the potency of this "Force." Activated by "Fame's posterior Trumpet" (4.71), force evidently exerts itself without any "guide" or external agent. It is "inert," "inward," "vast," "sure," and "transporting" (4.73–78). And it is exercised through "impulse," "attraction," and "gravity," inclining all its objects toward one "centre" (4.77). The purview of this force extends to all the would-be human beings in the realm of the poem—authors, publishers, patrons, politicians—of any age:

> The young, the old, who feel her inward sway,
> One instinct seizes, and transports away.
> None need a guide, by sure Attraction led,
> And strong impulsive gravity of Head:
> None want a place, for all their Centre found,
> Hung to the Goddess, and coher'd around.
> . . . .
> The gath'ring number, as it moves along,
> Involves a vast involuntary throng,
> Who gently drawn, and struggling less and less,
> Roll in her Vortex, and her pow'r confess. (4.73–84)

---

11. Ernan McMullin, *Newton on Matter and Energy* (Notre Dame, IN: University of Notre Dame Press, 1979), 35, 43.

The account of the powers that govern the dunces' attraction to "Dulness" here exactly recites the contemporary Newtonian account of gravitational force, using the same terms advanced by Newton—"attraction," "inertia," "impulse," "gravity," "centre." The poem dwells with, elaborates, and extends these powers across its human as well as its environmental/geological and cosmic entities and realms. The consequence is that all of these entities are systematically materialized—represented as subjected to gravitational force.

As to its purportedly human entities, *The Dunciad* as we have seen is famous for its numerous, specifically identified population of contemporary writers, the "dunces." Pope fills the poem with the names of his contemporaries—"Fools"—who as we have seen are listed and relisted by name, at every turn (1.136). For example, during the close of the sleeping contest at the end of book 2, seven writers are named in five lines: Susanna Centlivre, Pierre Motteux, Abel Boyer, William Law, Thomas Morgan, Bernard Mandeville, and Benjamin Norton Defoe:

> At last Centlivre felt her voice to fail,
> Motteux himself unfinish'd left his tale,
> Boyer the State, and Law the Stage gave o'er,
> Morgan and Mandevil could prate no more;
> Norton, from Daniel and Ostroea sprung,
> Bless'd with his father's front, and mother's tongue,
> Hung silent down his never-blushing head;
> And all was hush'd, as Folly's self lay dead. (2.411–18)

In effect, the poem designates these particular named authors only in order to repudiate their autonomy, their vitality, and their influence as individual animate human beings in the same verses: their voices "fail"; they disclaim their professions; and each of these named authors along with "all" they represent is "hush'd" in a state that would resemble death, were they actually living beings.

The "silence" of this population of authors is an ongoing refrain and an indication of the poem's renunciation of human vitality (2.417). These authors are also systematically displaced from the human through a kind of mingling with expressions of manifestations of the other-than-human. For example, in the following passage, particular names of contemporary authors—Benjamin

Norton Defoe, John Breval, and John Dennis—are indiscriminately mingled with the random sounds that instantiate the poem's representation of force, replacing the purported human referents of these names with the "pow'r of Noise" (2.222) and human vitality with the hyperactivity of "Dissonance" and "Interruption":

> Twas chatt'ring, grinning, mouthing, jabb'ring all,
> And Noise and Norton, Brangling and Breval,
> Dennis and Dissonance, and captious Art,
> And Snip-snap short, and Interruption smart. (2.236–39)

But the key locus in the poem for this materialization of individual animate human beings occurs in the extended account of Cibber's burning of his books in book 1. In a review of a full population of authors, each individual human being is designated through the representation of a bound book; by this means, animate human beings become objects. For the classical authors,

> But, high above, more solid Learning shone,
> The Classics of an Age that heard of none;
> There Caxton slept, with Wynkyn at his side,
> One clasp'd in wood, and one in strong cow-hide;
> There, sav'd by spice, like Mummies, many a year,
> Dry Bodies of Divinity appear:
> De Lyra there a dreadful front extends,
> And here the groaning shelves Philemon bends. (1.147–54)

The heavy, physical "Bodies" weighing down the bookshelves here are "dry," wooden or leather objects; they outlast the human life span "like Mummies," providing material kindling for the fire that Cibber will shortly light.

The Dunciad's images of bookshelves here reflect the poem's imbrication with the rise of the modern library and the archive of contemporary material culture. Harold Weber describes the poem's reflection of "the new age of libraries," including catalogs, book clubs, circulating libraries, and private collections, which were a vital concomitant to the rise of the printing industry.[12]

---

12. Harold Weber, "The 'Garbage Heap' of Memory: At Play in Pope's Archives of Dulness," *Eighteenth-Century Studies* 33 (1999): 4.

The poem makes material collections of books a pervasive feature of Dulness's realm—initially in Cibber's first appearance and his library-burning in book 1 and generally as an ongoing facet of the characterization of the dunces as walking libraries: "A Lumberhouse of books in ev'ry head, / For ever reading, never to be read!" (3.193–94). Weber argues that "the library emerges as one of the most powerful symbols of Dulness's triumph."[13] In the context of the inherent counterhuman force of matter represented in the poem, *The Dunciad*'s gatherings of things in libraries and archives offer another demonstration of that proliferative or cumulative counterenergy that paradoxically stands against or transforms the human.

Animation is the corollary effect here: the materialization of the human into the form of the book in turn animates the material thing, as the books then, themselves, achieve opportunities for "flight" and "light." In book 3, the same "Calf" or "cow-hide"-bound volumes "wing" away in their "new bodies" after their dipping in the waters of Lethe:

> Instant, when dipt, away they wing their flight,
> Where Brown and Mears unbar the gates of Light,
> Demand new bodies, and in Calf's array,
> Rush to the world, impatient for the day. (3.26–29)

These "rushing" books are released to the world by the contemporary publishers George Brown and William Mears, and human being is replaced by the "new" and "impatient" energy of the material thing. As Pope explains in his note to this passage, "the allegory of the souls of the dull coming forth in the forms of their books dressed in calf's leather, and being let abroad in vast numbers by Booksellers, is sufficiently intelligible"—"intelligible" as the effect of gravitational force on matter.

Meanwhile the operations of gravity extend across the world of the poem. Beyond the combustible, calf-skin bodies of the poem's other-than-human population, *The Dunciad* also systematically and dramatically materializes its geography and even its astronomy—a realization of Newtonian physics as a universal, cosmic force. In book 1, this environmental/geological scope is demonstrated as the force of Dulness is shown to "shift" and "turn" oceans and continents, climate, and seasons:

---

13. Weber, 4.

> How time himself stands still at her command,
> Realms shift their place, and Ocean turns to land.
> Here gay Description Aegypt glads with show'rs,
> Or gives to Zembla fruits, to Barca flowr's;
> Glitt'ring with ice here hoary hills are seen,
> There painted vallies of eternal green,
> In cold December fragrant chaplets blow,
> And heavy harvests nod beneath the snow. (1.71–78)

And while this force is upturning continents and waters, it can also "mold . . . a new World" (4.15) and configure stars and suns:

> Yon stars, yon suns, he rears at pleasure higher,
> Illumes their light, and sets their flames on fire. (3.259–60)

And it can then turn to engage the whole solar system:

> Thence a new world to Nature's laws unknown,
> Breaks out refulgent, with a heav'n its own:
> Another Cynthia her new journey runs,
> And other planets circle other suns.
> The forests dance, the rivers upward rise,
> Whales sport in woods, and dolphins in the skies. (3.240–46)

The Dunciad's ongoing engagement with force is thus systematically generalized across every object of representation in the poem, from the authors and publishers, the gentlemen on the "Grand Tour," the virtuosi, the patrons of the arts, or the politicians to the rivers and oceans, the valleys and deserts, and the suns and stars.

And like Newtonian gravitation, *The Dunciad*'s force happens outside of human agency. On the one hand, this power seems to be associated with the Mighty Mother, Dulness, who appears to preside over the activities in the poem and over the apocalypse of its ending. As if performing a human or royal role, Dulness is seated on a "Throne" (1.36), "rules" the mind (1.16), exercises "imperial sway" (3.123), and "anoints" a monarch (1.287). But on the other hand, systematically repudiating such imputations of human agency is Dulness's consistent removal from visibility, action, and eminence. Her majesty is invariably observed through "a veil of fogs" (1.262) or in "a Cloud conceal'd" (4.17). And likewise her own omniscience itself is such that she "beholds [only] thro' fogs" (1.180); she is "all-seeing [only in] mists" (4.469). In effect, the poem creates Dulness only to repudiate her activity as the human-like agent of the poem's force—referring that mysterious power outside of the figure of the Mighty Mother to pervasive, intangible effects like "the wond'rous pow'r of Noise" (2.222) or "music, rage, and mirth" (3.238) or to uncentered, distributed phenomena like "mobs" (1.67), "spawn" (1.59), "throngs" (4.82) or "crowds on crowds" (4.135). As we have seen, every object, scene, and entity in the poem is impelled by this distributed, pervasive power whose universal force is everywhere, while Dulness's seeming agency dissolves in "fogs" and gives way to "noise." *The Dunciad*'s theory of the force inherent in matter is universal in scope and exercises itself beyond, outside of, or counter to human agency.

II

Supplementary to this counterhuman representation of force, the scene of *The Dunciad* also disavows a human-generated system or process of hierarchy and order. On the one hand, the only word specifically and repeatedly proffered by the poem as an account of its other-than-human system seems to indicate an impossibility of order: "Chaos" (1.12). "Chaos," repeatedly referenced, characterizes Dulness's ancestral origin, serves as her nickname, and describes the world that Dulness beholds as she looks down from her throne: "the Chaos dark and deep" (1.55). But on the other hand, the systems and processes of the poem are characterized more specifically and fully than "chaos" can comprise. *The Dunciad* offers an ongoing and even insistent representation of intra-activity across the material forms that we have seen to be its population—authors, booksellers, books, dunces, rivers, lands, oceans, moons, and suns. Well beyond that initial assertion of chaos, the poem offers a complex repertory of relational indicators that quickly come to dominate its action. In effect, through this presentation of assemblages and processes, *The Dunciad* provides for an experiment in nonhierarchic, anti-anthropocentric, counterhuman theories of relationality. Like the new materialist approaches in physics, molecular biology, and vitalism reviewed earlier, *The Dunciad*, too, can be seen to explore concepts of entanglement, turbulence, chaos, intra-activity, flattening, and even cascading.

Almost every passage in the poem offers or implies an alternative scenario for process or relationality. We have already seen, in the poem's play with names and noise—"Noise and Norton, Brangling and Breval, / Dennis and Dissonance"—an assemblage of authors, or at least of authors' names, based on incoherent sound-making (2.236–37). But the base line for *The Dunciad*'s scenarios of relationality is set up through the poem's pervasive insistence on "numbers": hundreds, millions, mobs, or crowds—from the "hundred clenches" and the "Mob of Metaphors" at the beginning of the first book (1.63, 67) to the "hundred sons," the "millions and millions," and the "gath'ring numbers" that assemble throughout the poem (1.63, 3.31, 4.80) to the repeated convening of "thick and more thick" "crowds on crowds" of dunces (4.190, 135) that comprise the whole unfolding narrative of book 4. These hundreds and millions of things—objectified beings, books, genres, concepts, figures of speech, ranks, titles, insects, eggs, ripples, streams, sounds, yawns—are the raw materials of an extended poetic experiment in counterhuman relationality.

In the course of the poem, things may be assembled according to mixing, joining, listing, streaming, whirling, fires, storms, or even through sleeping. And each of these options is distinctively defined. For example, the operative linkage might arise from the intermediate space separating proximate objects—an intangible "betwixt"—which posits a relationship, though an undefinable one, "betwixt a Heiddegre and owl" (1.290). In the following passage, the space between authors ("'twixt") and the intermediacy of the production ("past"/ "future," "old"/"new") serve to describe this intermediate linkage of dunces:

> A past, vamp'd, future, old, reviv'd, new piece,
> 'Twixt Plautus, Fletcher, Shakespear, and Corneille,
> Can make a Cibber, Tibbald, or Ozell. (1.284–86)

Things may also be entangled through "linking" or "joining":

> Where Dukes and Butchers join to wreathe my crown,
> At once the Bear and Fiddle of the town. (1.218–19)

> Pluto with Cato thou for this shalt join,
> And link the Mourning Bride to Proserpine. (3.309–10)

Things may simply be assembled in lists, "side by side" or one after another, leveling or flattening the distinctions among them:

> There march'd the bard and blockhead, side by side,
> Who rhym'd for hire, and patroniz'd for pride.
> Narcissus, prais'd with all a Parson's pow'r,
> Look'd a white lily sunk beneath a show'r.
> There mov'd Montalto with superior air;
> His stretch'd-out arm display'd a Volume fair. (4.101–10)

> "Behold yon' Isle, by Palmers, Pilgrims trod,
> Men bearded, bald, cowl'd, uncowl'd, shod, unshod,
> Peel'd, patch'd, and piebald, linsey-wolsey brothers,
> Grave Mummers! sleeveless some, and shirtless others. (3.113–16)

Or things may be assembled through fluid forms of cascading—"mixing," "mingling," or "pouring":

>   an endless band
> Pours forth, and leaves unpeopled half the land.
> A motley mixture! in long wigs, in bags,
> In silks, in crapes, in Garters, and in rags. (2.219–22)

> [the water of Lethe] Pours into Thames: and hence the mingled wave
> Intoxicates the pert, and lulls the grave:
> There, all from Paul's to Aldgate drink and sleep. (2.343–45)

Or they may be assembled through fluid forms of turbulence: "whirling," "rushing," "conflagration," and "storm":

> Down, down they larum, with impetuous whirl,
> The Pindars, and the Miltons of a Curl. (3.163–64)

> All sudden, Gorgons hiss, and Dragons glare,
> And ten-horn'd fiends and Giants rush to war.
> Hell rises, Heav'n descends, and dance on Earth:
> Gods, imps, and monsters, music, rage, and mirth,
> A fire, a jigg, a battle, and a ball,
> 'Till one wide conflagration swallows all. (3.234–39)

> Immortal Rich! How calm he sits at ease
> 'Mid snows of paper, and fierce hail of pease;
> And proud his Mistress' orders to perform,
> Rides in the whirlwind, and directs the storm. (3.261–64)

And as the logical extension and imaginative realization of the inertia that defines this force, things may even be assembled through the positionality of sleeping, as we noted in the passage at the end of book 2 when Centlivre, Motteaux, Boyer, Law, Morgan, Mandevil, and Norton together all fall asleep: "And all was hush'd, as Folly's self lay dead" (2.418). But most conclusively, at the end of the poem, sleep brings all the materials of the contemporary world into the flattening relationality exerted by the force of "the Yawn of Gods": "Churches and Chapels," "Armies" and "Navies," "Right and Wrong," "*Wit*" and "*Art*," "Religion" and "Morality":

> Wide, and more wide, [the yawn] spread o'er all the realm;
> Ev'n Palinurus nodded at the Helm:
> The Vapour mild o'er each Committee crept;
> Unfinish'd Treaties in each Office slept;
> And Chiefless Armies doz'd out the Campaign;
> And Navies yawn'd for Orders on the Main.
> . . . .
> Thus at her felt approach, and secret might,
> *Art* after *Art* goes out, and all is Night.
> See skulking *Truth* to her old Cavern fled,
> Mountains of Casuistry heap'd o'er her head!
> *Philosophy*, that lean'd on Heav'n before,
> Shrinks to her second cause, and is no more. (4.613–18, 639–44)

These modes of relationality reiteratively work out the random consequences of the actions of gravitational force across the material world of the poem. And the final "chaos" with which the poem ends is inclusive of all the entities of that material world, including—as just one among many—the "*human*":

> Nor *public* Flame, nor *private*, dares to shine;
> Nor *human* Spark is left, nor Glimpse *divine*!
> Lo! thy dread Empire, Chaos! is restor'd;
> Light dies before thy uncreating word. (4.651–54)

The "*human*" is repeatedly assembled in relation to the material things of the poem as those things are "moved," "transported," and "shifted" by the vast, sure, inert force that pervades this counterhuman world. And then finally the "*human*" is "uncreated" by that "universal" force. By means of its engagement with gravitation, then, *The Dunciad* unleashes matter from notions of human order so as to reimagine not just the human itself but systems of hierarchy and relationality shaped by human being. The poem helps us ask the question of whether the counterhuman imaginary can propose a repudiation of the human, even from within the scenario of human creativity.

In fact and as we have seen, *The Dunciad*'s counterhuman imaginary is inextricable from the human-centered cultural imaginary—from human creativity and from the human literary canon. In that respect—inextricability—the counterhuman imaginary cannot directly repudiate the human. But *The Dunciad* does offer a metacaveat for human creativity that extends beyond its local representation of the other-than-human forms of vitality and the antihierarchical forms of relationality that we have documented in the poem. Through its engagement with the other-than-human, *The Dunciad* qualifies the assumption of the exclusive, inherent, supreme human power to create, adjudicate, or order. But it also warns us that we must draw back, as well, from the assumption that the poem's counterhuman vision reflects either an unmediated proximity with "real" matter—an assumption that we might naturally be tempted to project on the basis of the poem's connection with Newtonian physics—or, relatedly, some form of political efficacy or ethical judgment on "reality."

The political or the ethical—and the "real"—are, for some new materialist critics and for many environmental and animal studies critics, the ultimate rationale and even point of reference. In *Animals and Other People*, Heather Keenleyside sees literary representations of the other-than-human as making "real-world claims" about "cultural and intellectual debates that are still with us."[14] And Tobias Menely in *The Animal Claim* seeks to show that the animal "voice" as expressed in literary or political discourse involves a process of representation that includes a direct "claim

---

14. Heather Keenleyside, *Animals and Other People: Literary Forms and Living Beings in the Long Eighteenth Century* (Philadelphia: University of Pennsylvania Press, 2017), 1.

to rights" on the part of animals in the real world, which requires human action.[15] Sarah Ellenzweig and John Zammito's provocative summary account of new materialist methodology in their introduction to *The New Politics of Materialism* provides an overview of the terms of the investment by new materialism in this sort of "real-world" political claim: "new materialism invests in an ontology of vital matter in order to ensure new forms of political action and engagement." But they go on to suggest that the authority for that claim to a proximity to the "real" and for an articulation of ethical values and political demands is based on a reprojection of "human values onto nature": "New materialism's eagerness to extend agency to objects . . . does little to unsettle a uniquely human obsession with agency and its correlates—selfhood, rationality, choice, intention, mastery," and knowledge.[16]

Jane Bennett's representation of thing-power in *Vibrant Matter* demonstrates the same caveat as that suggested by Ellenzweig and Zammito's critique of the "uniquely human obsession with agency" and by *The Dunciad*'s imaginary world of gravitational force. In her introductory chapter, Bennett offers us a poetic scenario labeled "Debris":

> On a sunny Tuesday morning . . . in the grate over the
>   storm . . . there was:
> one large men's black plastic work glove
> one dense mat of oak pollen
> one unblemished dead rat
> one white plastic bottle cap
> one smooth stick of wood

Bennett goes on to represent these things as "stuff that commanded attention in its own right, as existents in excess of their association with human meanings, habits, or projects." Here is "thing-power," she suggests, which, just like Dulness's "uncreating word," "issued a call, even if I did not quite understand what it was saying."[17]

15. Tobias Menely, *The Animal Claim: Sensibility and the Creaturely Voice* (Chicago: University of Chicago Press, 2015), 6, 1.

16. Sarah Ellenzweig and John H. Zammito, "Introduction," in *The New Politics of Materialism: History, Philosophy, Science*, ed. Ellenzweig and Zammito (London: Routledge, 2017), 10.

17. Bennett, *Vibrant Matter*, 4.

Bennett highlights the "impossibility" of understanding this poem to debris, as she tries "impossibly, to name the moment of independence . . . possessed by things," "to attend to the it as actant."[18] The impossibility of Bennett's debris is another redaction of *The Dunciad*'s uncreating word; both impossible scenarios enable us to question—and to uncreate—human creative agency, even as the human witness focuses on the effort to represent the agency of matter.

III

Taking seriously this requirement to uncreate the human—to continue using *The Dunciad*'s version of the concept—requires a significant adjustment to the conceptual groundwork around current approaches to the other-than-human, particularly for literary animal studies and new materialism. The thing-work of *The Dunciad* might be seen as contrapuntal to the world-making of the cultural imaginary, as that concept has been developed in social theory and cultural criticism. Cornelius Castoriadis defines the "imaginary institution of society" as each society's "singular manner of living, of seeing and of conducting its own existence, its world, and its relations with this world."[19] The "uncreating" activity of *The Dunciad* suggests that that "singular existence" contains its own counterexistence, specifically if we attend to its intimacy with the evocation of the other-than-human. In fact, *The Dunciad* demonstrates that the human cultural imaginary is permeated by the counterhuman: it is a world-making consensus whose purview simultaneously includes those realms that are contrapuntal or even contradictory to the human, through processes of relationality not subject to human definition. Without claiming to use human power to endow matter with agency, the counterhuman imaginary opens an alternative site for the exploration of such agency, in an incommensurable relationship with the "singular existence" of human creativity.

---

18. Bennett, 3.

19. Cornelius Castoriadis, *The Imaginary Institution of Society*, trans. Karen Blamey (Cambridge, MA: MIT Press, 1987), 145. Originally published as *L'institution imaginaire de la société*, 1975.

In *The Dunciad*, this "singular existence" includes a powerful, integrated, encyclopedic synthesis of the development of the institutions of modern capitalism. The poem draws together and demonstrates the integration of a set of tropes that express the most vital elements of its historical moment: the leveling vitality of urban expansion, the capitalization and commodification of the printing industry, the volatility of credit and financial speculation, and the vision of an imperial British identity. In particular, the writers and booksellers that make up—simultaneously—the material and the human population of the poem are the local agents of capitalism for this historical moment. As I have argued elsewhere, this population expresses variously and concretely the fixation on profit and demand, the professionalization of authorship, the growth of productivity, and the focus on an expanding trade that define the capitalist development of an industry. Meanwhile, Dulness herself is a parodic manifestation of Britannia, the preeminent allegorical representative of the expansionist British nation; the scenes of Dulness on her throne echo the commonplace image of Britannia on contemporary English coinage; and the account of Dulness's vision across oceans and continents directly evokes current claims to British imperial power and global influence.[20]

What happens when capitalism encounters gravity? The material force that moves the counterhuman pulls the historical force of capitalism into the realm of the "impossible," into the scenario of "chaos" that for this poem, for Lucretian atomism, and for modern thermodynamics envisions a turbulence beyond Enlightenment humanist certainties and beyond human creativity:

> Thy hand, great Anarch! lets the curtain fall;
> And Universal Darkness buries All. (6.653–56)

The Dunciad teaches us to look for scenarios of uncertainty and impossibility in imaginative literature, as a means to an embedded analysis of the other-than-human. The methodology that we might project from our engagement with the other-than-human in this poem entails a movement from observations of materialization and of jarring incommensurability to an account of

---

20. Brown, *Fables of Modernity*, 137–42.

turbulence that puts that incommensurability into unconventional, impossible motion. These processes of relationality and turbulence are the point of no return for an analysis of the counterhuman imaginary; they leave the human reader in an indeterminate "Darkness" by repudiating all conventions of dis-cursive certainty and narrative conclusion, through the ongoing novelty of the "new Arms," "new light," and the "new world to Nature's laws unknown" (3.240).

Igreja de S. Paulo.   Eglise de S. Paul.

Figure 4. *Recueil des plus belles ruines de Lisbonne causes par le tremblement et par le feu du premier Novembre 1755. Eglise de S. Paul* (1757), by Jacques-Philippe Le Bas.

Chapter 4

"When Time Shall End"

Poetry of the Lisbon Earthquake

Earthquake has a distinctive status in the eighteenth-century repertory of literary accounts of the environmental realm through its consistent connection with apocalypse. A passage from the last section of a hymn on the 1755 Lisbon earthquake by Charles Wesley—titled "Hymn upon the pouring out of the Seventh Vial, *Rev.* xvi. xvii, &c. Occasioned by the Destruction of Lisbon" (1756)—supplies a biblically explicit example:

> The mighty Shock *seems now* begun,
>   Beyond Example great,
> And lo! the World's Foundations groan
>   As at their instant Fate!
> Jehovah shakes the shatter'd Ball,
>   Sign of the general Doom!
> The Cities of the Nations fall,
>   And *Babel's* Hour is come.[1]

---

1. Charles Wesley, *Hymns occasioned by the Earthquake, March 8, 1750. To which are added an hymn upon the pouring out of the seventh vial, . . . Occasioned by the destruction of Lisbon*, part 1,

And John Biddulph's *Poem on the Earthquake at Lisbon* (1755) concludes with a vision of the "last Earthquake":

> And when on opening of the Sixth great Seal,
> With her last Earthquake this round World shall reel,
> The Sun shall lose his Fires in endless Night,
> And the Moon turn'd to Blood, glare horrid Light,
> When Comets dire shall sweep athwart the Sky,
> And Stars like Leaves before the Tempest fly;
> When fervent Heat the Elements shall burn,
> And like a Furnace Earth to Ashes turn,
> And all the Heavens in that dreadful Day,
> Like to a Scroll roll'd up, shall pass away—[2]

Engagement with *earthquake* gives human creativity a singular, sudden, sizable, descriptive undertaking. That undertaking is highlighted in eighteenth-century literature by the particular experience of the Lisbon earthquake of 1755—understood by historical seismologists today to be "the largest documented seismic event to have affected Europe."[3] The poetry of the Lisbon earthquake thus offers a unique test case for counterhuman literary explication, since its engagement with the other-than-human entails a relative coherence both around a single event and around the distinctive nature of that event.

2nd ed. (London: E. Farley, 1756), 10. Subsequent references to this source are cited parenthetically in the text.

2. John Biddulph, *A Poem on the Earthquake at Lisbon* (London: W. Owen, 1755), ll. 241–50. Subsequent references to this source are cited parenthetically in the text.

3. David K. Chester, "The 1755 Lisbon Earthquake," *Progress in Physical Geography* 25 (2001): 383; citing J. Mezcua, J. Ruida, and J. M. Martínez Solares, "Seismicity of the Ibero-Maghrebian Region," in *Seismicity, Seismotectonics and Seismic Risk of the Ibero-Maghrebian Region*, ed. Mezcua and A. Udías (Madrid: Instituto Geografico Nacional, 1991), 17–28. See also, for recent detailed accounts of the Lisbon earthquake including contemporary reports as well as recent geological assessments, Jelle Zeilinga de Boer and Donald Theodore Sanders, *Earthquakes in Human History: The Far-Reaching Effects of Seismic Disruptions* (Princeton, NJ: Princeton University Press, 2005); T. D. Kendrick, *The Lisbon Earthquake* (London: Methuen, 1956); Nicholas Shrady, *The Last Day: Wrath, Ruin, and Reason in the Great Lisbon Earthquake of 1755* (New York: Penguin, 2008); and Edward Paice, *Wrath of God: The Great Lisbon Earthquake of 1755* (London: Quercus, 2008).

I

The Lisbon earthquake occurred in the morning of November 1, 1755, All Saints Day. Its three major shocks together lasted over ten minutes' time and were followed by many aftershocks. Projections of its intensity according to the modern magnitude scale (the Richter scale) vary from 8.5 to 9.5; the latter, if accurate, would make this the largest earthquake in human history.[4] The earthquake destroyed most of the city of Lisbon, ignited a weeklong fire, and was followed within two hours by three tsunamis of—at their highest— perhaps sixty feet, across the affected coastal areas. In Lisbon, these tsunamis overwhelmed the waterfront, sinking all but the largest vessels and carrying away coastal structures as well as the hundreds of people who had fled from the wreckage and fires in the city toward the Tagus River and the port. Beyond Lisbon, the earthquake caused major structural damage throughout southern Portugal, the Iberian Peninsula, Algiers, and elsewhere in northwestern Africa, and it was felt as well in Normandy, Brittainy, Switzerland, and northern Italy. Across its whole extent, this event is thought to have killed up to one hundred thousand people. In Lisbon ten thousand people were killed and forty to fifty thousand injured—these casualties probably affecting 40 percent of the city's population.[5]

The Lisbon earthquake generated a discursive response that stands out in the history of the human engagement with the experiences of other earthquakes. Theodore E. D. Braun and John B. Radner note in their introductory overview of their collection on responses to this event that "it had a profound effect on European thinking for well over 100 years; and because the event made such an impact on the consciousness of people living at the time, it still remains potent in the European imagination."[6] And Jean-Paul Poirier in his review of the scientific, literary, and philosophical reactions to the earthquake concludes that "in the present age, no natural catastrophe could elicit the same amount of literary, theological and philosophical productions,

---

4. Chester, "1755 Lisbon Earthquake," table 3, 370.
5. See especially Chester; Kendrick, *Lisbon Earthquake*; Shrady, *Last Day*; and Paice, *Wrath of God*.
6. Theodore E. D. Braun and John B. Radner, introduction to *The Lisbon Earthquake of 1755: Representations and Reactions*, ed. Braun and Radner (Oxford, UK: Voltaire Foundation, 2005), 3.

as the Lisbon earthquake."[7] This distinctiveness is shaped in part by the historical coincidence of the earthquake with a set of transformations or tensions that mark this moment in eighteenth-century European history. Struggles and debates around the Reformation intersect with earthquake observers' consistent engagement with religion. The visibility of the city and harbor of Lisbon as a center of European maritime expansion make the destruction there singularly significant, as an intrusion upon the ideologies of colonial and imperial expansion. And, as we shall see, the scope of human suffering in this geologic event intersects with key issues for Enlightenment humanism and optimism.

The immediate popular consensus expressed in England and very broadly across Europe was that the earthquake was an act of divine retribution—a view that is explicit throughout the literary representations of the earthquake as well as in the many topical sermons and religious publications of the moment. Charles Wesley's "Hymn 2" in his *Hymns occasioned by the Earthquake* makes this impact most explicit, though this assumption is relevant throughout the English earthquake poetry:

> JESUS, LORD, to whom we cry,
>   The true Repentance give,
>   Give us at thy Feet to lie,
>   And tremble, and believe;
>   On the Rock of Ages place
> Our Souls, 'till all the Wrath is o'er,
>   Ground, and 'stablish us in Grace,
>   And Bid us sin no more. (3)

The designations of the rationale for God's wrath, however, varied diametrically—from punishment for the bloody crimes of the Inquisition, which was still a powerful force in eighteenth-century Portugal, on the one hand, to retribution for the excessive tolerance shown to the heretics in Lisbon, on the other. For example, in "Poem on the Late Earthquake at Lisbon" (1755), it is the "Savage Hearts" of the Inquisitors that attract the earthly "Thunders" of "Heaven's Justice":

---

7. Jean-Paul Poirier, "The 1755 Lisbon Disaster: The Earthquake That Shook Europe," *European Review* 14 (2006): 180.

A murderous Crew within his Kingdoms dwell,
Ally'd to Satan and the Fiends in Hell;
To mild Religion, Honour, Mercy Foes,
All Laws divine as human overthrows:
. . . .
The Rack, the Torture, is to them a Joy,
Their Aim to plunder, threaten and destroy;
Jews, *Turks*, or *Christians* serve their impious Turn,
Each, like a Faggot, undistinguished Burn;
. . . .
But Heaven's high Will who looks on Man's Offence,
And with due Weight his Justice can dispense;
Who views Mankind with an Omniscient Ray,
And see's Tomorrow as he see's To-day;
Oft bids his loud impending Thunders Roll,
To strike a Terror in the guilty Soul.[8]

In London, the Lisbon earthquake was preceded in February 1750 by an earthquake of a magnitude of about 2.6, centered directly under the city; this quake killed two people and resulted in minor damage, but it created extensive anxiety in and beyond the city and was understood as a divine warning—today's seismologists also understand this event as a warning since it indicated the presence of an active fault under central London. This quake generated a lively response of sermons and religious tracts and seemed, retrospectively, to presage the Lisbon earthquake. Wesley's collection *Hymns occasioned by the Earthquake, March 8, 1750*, was published—following the Lisbon earthquake—in a second edition in 1756 along with the "Hymn upon the Pouring out of the Seventh Vial . . . Occasioned by the Destruction of Lisbon."[9] And upon news of the Lisbon earthquake, a royal decree was made for a Fast Day across England to promote general

---

8. "A Poem on the Late Earthquake at Lisbon. To which is added, Thoughts in a Church-Yard" (London: R. and J. Dodsley, [1755]), 4. Subsequent references to this source are cited parenthetically in the text.

9. For a perspective on Charles Wesley's hymns and on both Charles Wesley's and John Wesley's responses to the earthquakes in London and Lisbon, see Robert Webster, "The Lisbon Earthquake: John and Charles Wesley Reconsidered," in Braun and Radner, *Lisbon Earthquake of 1755*, 116–26.

repentance and, through that penitence and prayer, to prevent further cataclysm.[10]

Earthquake writing—including eyewitness accounts, sermons, and poetry—reflects what Christopher Weber has termed "disaster discourse," which is "comprised of overlapping rhetorical and narrative devices [including a] foregrounded speechlessness [that] triggers an array of highly stylized descriptions that have been recycled over and over for centuries." These conventions highlight "the screams of dying people, the trampling of the dead, distressed mothers cradling their children, and the scandalous sight of improperly dressed people."[11] In Biddulph's *Poem on the Earthquake at Lisbon*, for example,

> Husbands are here seen pressing thro' the Throng,
> Nor know they drag their clinging Wives along.
> Coy Virgins of their Lovers once afraid,
> Now hang on Strangers Necks and court their Aid.
> And there a ghastly Group of women see!
> A Picture of the Ghosts they soon must be,
> Wringing their Hands, sad solemn Silence keep,
> While Infants wonder why their Mothers weep. (ll. 53–60)

And similarly in Henry Kett's "An Episode Taken from a Poem on the Earthquake at Lisbon" (1793),

> Th' impatient sailors waiting for Augustus
> Repulse the gathering multitudes escap'd
> From recent havock; tottering age and youth,
> The rich, the indigent, distracted mothers
> And weeping children, urg'd by common fear,
> To the same spot repair'd; with arms extended
> To Heaven, they beg for swift deliverance
> From coming fate; or frantic and forlorn

---

10. See Poirier, "1755 Lisbon Disaster," 176; and Robert G. Ingram, "'The trembling Earth is God's Herald': Earthquakes, Religion and Public Life in Britain during the 1750s," in Braun and Radner, *Lisbon Earthquake of 1755*, 113.

11. Christopher Weber, "Tableaux of Terror: The Staging of the Lisbon Earthquake of 1755 as Cathartic Spectacle," in *Catastrophe and Catharsis: Perspectives on Disaster and Redemption in German Culture and Beyond*, ed. Katharina Gerstenberger and Tanja Nusser (Rochester, NY: Camden House, 2015), 19, 26.

> With streaming eyes gaz'd on the gloomy ocean,
> Imploring every ship that rode the waves,
> To snatch them from the perils of the land.[12]

And in "A Poem on the Late Earthquake at Lisbon,"

> The People shriek with Terror and Dismay,
> Earth opes her Mouth and shuts them from the Day;
> Young lisping Babes around their Mothers cling,
> As tender Broods beneath the fostering Wing;
> Where is my Father? with a Look most mild,
> Or where my Mother? cries the duteous Child;
> Oh! spare them both, if one of us must dye
> T'appease the Anger of the Deity;
> Thy prostrate Servant graciously receive,
> Content to dye, but let my Parents live. (5)

Weber tracks the genealogy of these conventional images to the chronicles of the Roman historians and links them then to the repeated disaster scenes of sensationalist sixteenth-century broadsheets: "A comparative look at disaster narratives from the eighteenth century and the early modern period reveals that the descriptive details of the terror tableaux are interchangeable and not tied to a specific spatiotemporal context."[13]

The classical rhetorical device of *ponere ante oculos* (placing before the eyes) is the core resource for these accounts, and Helena Carvalhão Buescu explores these interchangeable "terror tableaux" through their use of visual imagery. The impulse to visualize that is inherent in "disaster discourse"—as Buescu explains—"inevitably results in an evident pathos quite easily identifiable through the melodramatic forms that are used to appeal to the reader (transformed as we have seen into an imaginary spectator). . . . This quality of putting on a terrible show, presented as such to the spectator, suddenly turns the city of Lisbon into an enormous stage where all spectators become actors too."[14]

---

12. Henry Kett, "An Episode Taken from a Poem on the Earthquake at Lisbon," in *Juvenile Poems* (Oxford, 1793), 47.

13. Weber, "Tableaux of Terror," 26.

14. Helena Carvalhão Buescu, "Seeing Too Much: The 1755 Earthquake in Literature," *European Review* 14 (2006): 333.

In regard to the formal interchangeability across these instances of "disaster discourse," then, the poetry of the Lisbon earthquake lacks specificity; the other-than-human event—even at 9.6 on the Richter scale—seems to escape the human imagination. The formal conventions of "disaster discourse" entail, in Buescu's words, "the capacity to construct the earthquake as the staging of a spectacle whose excessive dimension also becomes a guarantee of its persuasive and redemptive effect."[15] That is, the human cultural imaginary offers a symbolic scenario whose overdetermination obscures the other-than-human realm, presenting *earthquake* through a formal system that renders its meaning accessible, indisputable, and even practical for the human audience, as a warning or prevision of the Apocalypse.

II

Unlike the advances in the modern science of meteorology that were generated by the responses to the great storm of 1703, the 1755 Lisbon earthquake did not give rise to significant changes in the long-standing notion—from classical times—that explained both earthquakes and volcanoes as arising from the impact of subterranean winds or gases that were ignited through exposure to flammable substances. Jean-Paul Poirier describes Aristotle's theory in the *Meteorologics* of "windy exhalations," noting that "at the end of the eighteenth century, the prevailing scientific explanation of earthquakes still did not essentially differ from the Aristotelian pneumatic theory—only the subterranean winds were now thought to be gases produced by the 'fermentation,' followed by combustion and explosion, of flammable substances such as bitumen, sulphur, or nitre, found in the underground. This theory, promoted by Buffon among others, accounted nicely for the association of volcanoes with earthquakes."[16]

The same conclusion is drawn by Immanuel Kant in his 1756 *History and description of the most remarkable events relative to the earthquake that shook a great part of the earth at the end of the year 1755*, based on the notion of the flammable matter contained in the caverns of the earth. Poirier concludes that "the scientific impact of the Lisbon earthquake was insignificant; the

---

15. Buescu, 334–35.
16. Poirier, "1755 Lisbon Disaster," 174.

venerable pneumatic theories were trotted out and there were no geologists that could make field observations." But he notes that the prediction of a future earthquake in Lisbon, based on extrapolation from the historical interval, led to a surprisingly accurate result:

> Pedegache [Miguel Tibério Pedegache Brandão Ivo, a Portuguese eyewitness and correspondent of the *Journal Etranger*], in a book on the earthquake published in 1756, listed all earthquakes having struck Lisbon in historical times and noticed that the three greatest happened in 1309, 1531 and 1755, separated by intervals of 222 and 224 years. He then ventured a hypothesis, which, he says, "may seem extravagant to many people, but is nevertheless not without any foundation. It is that there will be a great earthquake in Portugal between 1977 and 1985." There, indeed, was one of magnitude 7.9 in 1969. Not bad for an extravagant hypothesis![17]

On the other hand, the 1755 Lisbon earthquake had a very visible and even momentous impact on Enlightenment thought, including Voltaire's responses, his exchange with Rousseau, and the aftermath of that conversation but extending to the broader debates around optimism and providential benevolence across the continent and in England. Voltaire's 1755 "Poem on the Lisbon Disaster: *an Inquiry into the Maxim, 'Whatever is, is Right'*" uses the events of the earthquake to refute the bold assertion of the benevolence of providence in Alexander Pope's *Essay on Man* (1732–34). Here is Pope's famously direct claim:

> All Nature is but Art, unknown to thee;
> All Chance, Direction, which thou canst not see;
> All Discord, Harmony not understood;
> All partial Evil, universal Good:
> And, spite of Pride, in erring Reason's spite,
> One truth is clear, "Whatever is, is RIGHT."[18]

Voltaire uses the enumeration of scenes of human suffering in the Lisbon earthquake as an obvious case in point and direct refutation of Pope's

---

17. Poirier, 174–75.

18. Alexander Pope, *An Essay on Man*, in *Poetry and Prose of Alexander Pope*, ed. Aubrey Williams (Boston: Houghton Mifflin, 1969), ep. 1, 289–94.

optimism, notably citing among other "terror tableaux" those deaths of infants that we have seen to be one of the key tropes of "disaster discourse":

> Women and children heaped up mountain high,
> Limbs crushed which under ponderous marble lie;
> Wretches unnumbered in the pangs of death,
> Who mangled, torn, and panting for their breath,
> Buried beneath their sinking roofs expire,
> And end their wretched lives in torments dire.
> Say, when you hear their piteous, half-formed cries,
> Or from their ashes see the smoke arise,
> Say, will you then eternal laws maintain,
> Which God to cruelties like these constrain?
> Whilst you these facts replete with horror view,
> Will you maintain death to their crimes was due?
> And can you then impute a sinful deed
> To babes who on their mothers' bosoms bleed?[19]

Voltaire's "Poem on the Lisbon Disaster" was followed in 1759 by *Candide; or, Optimism*, which can be understood broadly as the next stage in Voltaire's satire on the philosophy of benevolence. The proliferative misfortunes endlessly besetting Candide and his fellows throughout the narrative are encyclopedic with regard to their motivating frames of reference—including political, religious, social, colonial, romantic, and simply accidental contexts. Significantly, however, the Lisbon earthquake and the storm that immediately precedes it are the only representation of *Candide*'s engagement with environmental and geologic forces. At the outset of the narrative, within two chapters of his opening expulsion from the "earthly paradise" of Baron Thunder-ten-Tronckh's country seat, Candide and his companions find themselves in the Lisbon harbor: "After escaping the storm . . . [they] felt the earth tremble beneath them. The sea boiled up in the harbour and broke the ships which lay at anchor. Whirlwinds of flame and ashes covered the streets and squares. Houses came crashing down. Roofs toppled onto their foundations, and the foundations crumbled. Thirty thousand men, women and children were crushed to death under the

---

19. Voltaire and William F. Fleming, "The Lisbon Earthquake," *New England Review* 26 (2005): 186. Subsequent references to this source are cited parenthetically in the text.

ruins."[20] This trembling, boiling, crashing, crumbling, and crushing gives Pangloss—Candide's optimistic philosopher-companion who is shortly to be hanged by the Inquisition—the opportunity to repeat the narrative's absurd, satiric refrain:

> Pangloss consoled them with the assurance that things could not be otherwise:
> "For all this," said he, "is a manifestation of the rightness of things, since if there is a volcano at Lisbon it could not be anywhere else. For it is impossible for things not to be where they are, because everything is for the best."[21]

In *Candide*, the enumeration of scenes of suffering or "terror tableaux" that we have seen to be a central device of the earthquake poetry is extrapolated to the ironic or even ridiculous enumeration of unfortunate events that entirely constitute Voltaire's narrative. But all of these multiplying misfortunes are initiated by the geologic event of the Lisbon earthquake.

The earthquake has multiplier effects beyond *Candide*. Rousseau's response to Voltaire's "Poem on the Lisbon Disaster" in his *Lettre à M. de Voltaire* (August 18, 1756), and the debate that attached to the exchange between the two thinkers, fundamentally shaped ongoing discussions of providence, necessity, suffering, and inequality for a century to come.[22] Though Rousseau's modulations of Voltaire's critique were partial and even tentative— for instance, the suggestion that some of the victims of the earthquake may have been spared worse sufferings—according to José O. A. Marques, Rousseau's approach to the earthquake also offers a distinctive new perspective that prefigures modern notions of social vulnerability:

> Even if his attempted defense of Providence was in the end doomed to fail, Rousseau called attention to something that was not properly recognized until much later: the fact that social and behavioral patterns have a large influence in the occurrence of catastrophes that affect large human groups and which were until then blamed only on nature's whims. As it happened

---

20. Voltaire, *Candide; or, Optimism*, trans. John Butt (London: Penguin, 1947), 23, 33.

21. Voltaire, 35.

22. See José O. A. Marques, "The Paths of Providence: Voltaire and Rousseau on the Lisbon Earthquake," *Cadernos de História e Filosofia da Ciência* (CLE-Unicamp) 15 (2005): 33–57; and Russell R. Dynes, "The Dialogue between Voltaire and Rousseau on the Lisbon Earthquake: The Emergence of a Social Science View," *International Journal of Mass Emergencies and Disasters* 18 (2000): 97–115.

in so many other fields of investigation to which Rousseau made pioneer contributions, we see here the first tentative steps towards a sociological theory of disasters and the modern concept of vulnerability, with the associated notion of the State's responsibility in the prevention of such occurrences.[23]

The impacts of the representation of the 1755 Lisbon earthquake on human thinking, human modes of representation, and even human approaches to politics and society are profound. And significantly these impacts are framed as we have seen by the inherent interchangeability of "disaster discourse," which shapes *earthquake* according to human convention.

III

But while the conventional format of "disaster discourse" seems to place the other-than-human beyond human representation, it also provides for a counterhuman itinerary, corollary to the facets of the counterhuman imaginary that this study identifies elsewhere in the eighteenth-century imaginative engagement with the other-than-human. In the earthquake poetry, the conventional enumeration of suffering human beings—or those humans who are about to suffer—itself provides a starting point for a counterhuman explication, aligned with the autonomous multiplicities of Crusoe's proliferating objects and with the assemblages of "hundreds" and "millions" of beings, books, things, insects, and yawns of *The Dunciad*'s sustained experiment with relationality: "Behold an hundred sons, and each a Dunce."[24] Biddulph's *Poem on the Earthquake at Lisbon* here provides a corollary to *The Dunciad*'s assemblage of "hundreds" of beings:

> Down from on high the shatter'd Tacklings rush,
> And big with rattl'ing Ruin Thousands crush.
> There gapes the vast Abyss with hideous Roar,
> And in its Entrails swallows Thousands more. (ll. 85–88)

---

23. Marques, "Paths of Providence," 18.

24. Alexander Pope, *The Dunciad*, in *Poetry and Prose of Alexander Pope*, 3.138. Subsequent references to this source are cited parenthetically in the text.

These "thousands" or "hundreds" evoke an indiscriminate assemblage that is notably repeated across the poems on the Lisbon earthquake. *A Poem on the Late Earthquake at Lisbon* also describes the fate of the "hundreds" who had sought safety:

> Regardless of the kind hymnenial Tye,
> Distracted Husbands from their Conforts fly;
> Wives careless leave their tender Charge behind,
> And vainly seek a safe Retreat to find;
> . . . .
> Hundreds the gaping Chasms now destroys,
> Quells every Hope, and every Bliss annoys. (p. 5)

And Richard Clarke's "On an Earthquake" (1773) describes "ten thousand, thousand" of the dying:

> The lofty domes, man's fort and pride,
> And gorgeous tow'rs on every side,
>   In dust all humbled fall;
> Ten thousand, thousand, horrid cries
> Of dying mortals rend the skies
>   Who late for mercy call.[25]

These innumerable "thousands" are visible both in the scenes of the dying and also often in the accounts describing the diverse numerousness of the population of the city of Lisbon before the earthquake strikes. In Biddulph's *Poem on the Earthquake at Lisbon*, numerousness has an ongoing persistence from outset to apocalypse, as the poem opens with the same evocation of innumerable human beings who are later seen to perish in the "gaping Chasms"—in this case the crowds enjoying the city in the moments before the earthquake:

> Within the Town gay Crowds were seen to stray,
> While full Processions grac'd the festive Day.
> Mechanicks by their honest Labour fed,

---

25. Richard Clarke, "On an Earthquake, from a serious musical entertainment," in *The Nabob: Or, Asiatic Plunderers . . . to Which Are Annexed, A Few Fugitive Pieces of Poetry* (London: J. Townsend, 1773), 48. Subsequent references to this source are cited parenthetically in the text.

> With cheerful Visage earn'd their daily Bread;
> Misers were counting o'er their ill-got Store,
> But not contented meditating more.
> Spendthrifts were just awak'd from Golden Dreams;
> Projectors were inventing Lottery Schemes;
> Merchants were storing Goods from *India* brought;
> Clients were selling Lands which Lawyers bought.
> Behold a Youth, and sitting by his Side,
> A Damsel new-betroth'd, his destin'd Bride;
> Around them throngs a Train of Virgins gay,
> Preparing Garments for the Marriage-day. (ll. 15–28)

The discourse of enumeration displayed here bears a notable resemblance to the ongoing counterhuman experiment with assemblage that we have seen to characterize *The Dunciad*'s encounter with other-than-human chaos, from the many manifestations of multiplicity in book 1 of that poem—"Here one poor word an hundred clenches makes, / And ductile dullness new meanders takes" (1.63–64)—to the "crowds" that convene for Dullness' conferring of degrees in book 4:

> The gath'ring number as it moves along,
> Involves a vast involuntary throng,
> Who gently drawn, and struggling less and less,
> Roll in her vortex, and her pow'r confess.
> . . . .
> Now crowds on crowds around the Goddess press,
> Each eager to present the first Address.
> . . . .
> Prompt at the call, around the Goddess roll
> Broad hats, and hoods, and caps, a sable shoal:
> Thick and more thick the black blockade extends,
> A hundred head of Aristotle's friends (4.81–84, 135–36, 189–92)

Like *The Dunciad*, the earthquake poetry steps outside of human coherence and hierarchy through multiplication.

Meanwhile, however, in a kind of counterhuman oxymoron, this multiplication is often juxtaposed with an insistent projection of singularity or immediacy. In Biddulph's poem, for instance, the "Thousands" suddenly become "one":

> Horror and Desolation cou'd no more!
> And now that once fair Town with all her Store,
> And ev'ry Soul that hail'd the rising Day,
> Heaving in Death like one vast Body lay. (ll. 105–8)

Wesley's "Psalm XLVI" in his *Hymns occasioned by the Earthquake* names this singularity as "Earth's inmost Center" (8). And "On the Late Earthquake" offers a similar account of the Earth itself—at the moment of the earthquake, which suddenly becomes a single, integral, consuming being:

> When lo! a dreadful Sound affrights the Ear,
> As if portending Desolation near;
> The fatal noise th' astonish'd Sense surprise,
> And seems to rend the Concave of the Skies;
> A fierce Convulsion shakes the Womb of Earth,
> As if her Bowels sought a second Birth;
> . . . .
> The People shriek with Terror and Dismay,
> Earth opes her Mouth and shuts them from the Day. (5)

This sudden singularity is a persistent effect of the earthquake poetry, often signaled by a "fatal noise" or "roar" and characterized in terms of parts of the female human anatomy. In Biddulph's poem, again, "Earth's Womb was heard to groan with hollow Roar" (l. 47), or "Winds, Flames and Sulphur in her Bowels lurk" (l. 177).

To some extent, the counterhuman oxymoron that contrasts numerousness with singularity is representing a turn to the ultimate unity of the deity, to whose wrath the event of the earthquake is conventionally attributed. But even Wesley's *Hymns* project a powerful image of a singularity that is distinct from the biblical conventions of the trinity. "Hymn 1" begins and ends with the unity of the "Great God . . . the God of Love" but reflects the earthquake itself distinctively as a singular "Mouth": "The staggering Earth had yawn'd, and clos'd / Its Mouth on its devoted prey" (2). "Hymn 3" juxtaposes the numerousness of "The Crowd, the poor unthinking Crowd" with, "If Earth its Mouth *must* open wide, / To swallow up its Prey" (5). And in "Hymn 5," this powerful "Center" is linked directly with a sudden, emphatic evocation of immediacy—*"now"*:

> The Pillars of the Earth are thine,
>   And Thou hast set the World thereon;
> They at thy threatning Look incline,
>   The Center trembles at thy Frown,
> The everlasting Mountains bow,
> And GOD is in the Earthquake *now!* (7)

Immediacy is a facet of singularity, as is evident in this description, in Richard Clarke's poem, of the "sudden" "moment" of the earthquake, arising from the ruin of the "whole":

> Sudden the change, the change how great!
> A moment sinks that pride and state,
>   The whole in ruin falls:
> Hark! what a dreadful hollow sound
> From Earth's torn bowels shake the ground
>   And bursts the strongest walls. (47)

And this immediacy is also expressed in the present-tense evocation of earthquake-apocalypse and ensuing "new Creation" in Charles Wesley's hymn "Rev. xvi, xvii, &c.":

> So be it: Let this System end,
>   This ruinous Earth and Skies,
> The new *Jerusalem* descend,
>   The new Creation rise:
> Thy Power omnipotent assume,
>   Thy brightest Majesty,
> And when Thou dost in Glory come,
>   My LORD, remember me! (12)

Even as this poetry cites divine omnipotence, the disorienting collision of multiplicity and singular immediacy disorients human explanation, order, and even temporality.

IV

As we have seen, the human cultural imaginary constructs the Lisbon earthquake as a spectacle of suffering through iterative forms of "disaster discourse" that guide the reader to the lesson of repentance. But *earthquake*—the other-than-human geologic event that transformed the Earth in 1755—finds different, contrapuntal modes of representation in this poetry. A counterhuman excess or immeasurability or immediacy of *earthquake* is registered in this poetry's persistent engagement with a kind of autonomous multiplicity, which confounds orderly human hierarchy or systematic human coherence. *Multiplicity* is a feature of the counterhuman imaginary that this study has identified in a range of eighteenth-century texts. In *The Dunciad*, as we have seen in chapter 3, the many forms of multiplicity that proliferate across the universe of the poem create an ongoing engagement with interrelationality, an "impossible" radical aliveness that empowers the ultimate "creation" of a nonhierarchic, antianthropocentric expression of "chaos." Chapter 2 argues that in *Robinson Crusoe* the proliferation of objects is a signal of the "inexpressible" energy of matter on its own as it populates the "desert" island. And in chapter 1, in the comparison of the circulation narrative and the lapdog lyric, we found multiplicity to be equated with unexpected and unmeasurable cross-species and transbeing affect or "love"—that is, with distinctive modes of affinity that stand outside conventional human-based ontology. Here in the earthquake poetry also, multiplicity highlights proliferation in a way that points beyond human understanding or that surrenders human comprehension to an indescribable realm beyond the human.

And meanwhile, the oxymoron that we have observed in this poetry, in which the multiplicity of unnumbered human sufferers is juxtaposed with a powerful and sudden singularity and immediacy—either attributed to the deity or embedded in the earth itself—offers another moment of incongruity that eludes human conventions of coherence. The suddenness and immediacy of the collision between "ten thousand, thousand" and "the Earthquake *now*" is a counterhuman effect that points toward a transformative power inaccessible through "disaster discourse."

Voltaire's "Poem on the Lisbon Disaster" explicitly reproduces a version of this oxymoron in a reflective couplet that juxtaposes multiple "woes" with a singular, coherent, "general" "bliss":

> Yet in this direful chaos you'd compose
> A general bliss from individuals' woes. (189)

But in this case, the incongruity of the juxtaposition serves as a critique of the conventional earthquake poetry's defense of providential benevolence, a project that we have seen to be the core intention of Voltaire's poem. Here the attack on "philosophy" for seeking, oxymoronically, to generate "bliss" from individual "woes" is directly expressed:

> Horrors on horrors, griefs on griefs must show,
> That man's the victim of unceasing woe,
> And lamentations which inspire my strain,
> Prove that philosophy is false and vain. (186)

In fact, Voltaire's *earthquake* absorbs the counterhuman effects of the other earthquake poetry into its critique of optimism. Voltaire's "Lisbon Disaster" begins, as we have seen, with an extended rendering of the established conventions of "disaster discourse," just like the other earthquake poetry: "Women and children heaped up mountain high, / . . . Wretches unnumbered in the pangs of death, / . . . babes who on their mothers' bosoms bleed." (186). But the poem then explicitly targets that multiplicity, which we have seen as an indication of the impact of the counterhuman imaginary in the other earthquake poetry, as a "proof" that "philosophy is false and vain" (186).

Significantly, in this couplet attacking the problematic juxtaposition of a singular "bliss" with multiple "individuals' woes," Voltaire's poem names the event in question: "this . . . chaos." "Chaos" serves here as the term for that immediate indescribable moment that arises both through the counterhuman oxymoron of the other earthquake poetry and also from Voltaire's poem's revisionist attempt to absorb that counterhuman effect into the human imagination in despite of "philosophy": "chaos" expresses the incongruous, sudden impact of a singular power from accounts of multiplicity and despite the dissonant citation of "philosophy." We have seen this impact and this power in the ultimate counterhuman effect of *The Dunciad*. Here *The Dunciad*'s "chaos" helps to explicate Voltaire's "chaos" and its absorption of the counterhuman imaginary of the other earthquake poetry:

> —the all-composing Hour
> Resistless falls: The Muse obeys the Pow'r.
> She comes! she comes! the sable Throne behold
> Of *Night* Primæval, and of *Chaos* old!

. . . .
Philosophy, that lean'd on Heav'n before,
Shrinks to her second cause, and is no more.

. . . .
Lo! thy dread Empire, CHAOS! is restor'd;
Light dies before thy uncreating word. (4.627–30, 643–44, 653–54)

Reading the other-than-human *earthquake* across the earthquake poetry connects Voltaire's "chaos" and Pope's. For both texts, multiplicity repudiates conventions of order, consolation, and philosophy. In both poems, that repudiation reveals a new realm—in Voltaire's poem, a realm of "dire contention" that "overthrows" "all systems" (189, 191);[26] in Pope's poem, an entropy of "discontinuity, multiplicity and contingency."[27]

The "new world" of Pope's *Dunciad* is the *earthquake* of Voltaire's "Lisbon Disaster."

---

26. Here Voltaire is citing Pierre Bayle:

What do I learn from Bayle, to doubt alone?
Bayle, great and wise, all systems overthrows,
Then his own tenets labors to oppose. (191)

27. David Webb and William Ross, introduction to *The Birth of Physics*, by Michel Serres, trans. Webb and Ross (Lanham, MD: Rowman and Littlefield, 2018), 2 (originally published 1977).

THE STORM AT KENTISH-TOWN, ON TUESDAY.

Figure 5. *The Storm at Kentish Town* (1849), from *Illustrated London News.*
Image © London Metropolitan Archives (City of London).

Chapter 5

Storms and Torrents

Swift's "A City Shower" and Defoe's The Storm

The human narrators of Jonathan Swift's "A Description of a City Shower" (1710) and Daniel Defoe's *The Storm; or, A Collection of the Most Remarkable Casualties and Disasters Which Happen'd in the Late Dreadful Tempest Both by Sea and Land* (1704) cannot resist asserting their authority in the context of the representation of forces far beyond human control. The "careful [human] observers" evoked in the opening lines of Swift's "City Shower" are full of advice and "sure prognostics":

> Careful Observers may foretel the Hour
> (By sure Prognostics) when to dread a Show'r:
> . . . .
> If you be wise, then go not far to Dine,
> You'll spend in Coach-hire more than save in Wine.[1]

---

1. Jonathan Swift, "A Description of a City Shower," in *Swift: Poetical Works*, ed. Herbert Davis (London: Oxford University Press, 1967), 91–93, ll. 1–8. Subsequent references to this source are cited parenthetically in the text by line number.

And the journalist-narrator of *The Storm*—aka Defoe himself—asserts at the outset of the narrative the enduring authority of this "Book" of "Stories," even though the accounts he reproduces from his "Relators" "may in their own nature seem incredible": "a Book printed is a Record; remaining in every Man's Possession, always ready to renew its Acquaintance with his Memory, and always ready to be produc'd as an Authority or Voucher to any Reports he makes out of it, and conveys its Contents for Ages to come, to the Eternity of mortal Time, when the Author is forgotten in his Grave."[2]

But in both "A City Shower" and *The Storm*, these human assertions of authority in regard to the representation of environmental events immediately meet their counterhuman match. In "A City Shower," the human prognosticator gives place, in the following two couplets, first to a contemplative other-than-human being (a "pensive cat") and then to a disembodied vapor (a "stink"):

> While Rain depends, the pensive Cat gives o'er
> Her Frolicks, and pursues her Tail no more.
> Returning Home at Night, you'll find the Sink
> Strike your offended Sense with double Stink. (ll. 3–6)

This juxtaposition of human authority with distinctive other-than-human interventions effects a demotion or even a replacement of the human at the very outset of the poem and projects an ironic perspective backward on the orderly human confidence of the poem's authoritative opening citation of "careful observers."

And meanwhile, already throughout the preface to *The Storm*, the narrator's authority is pervasively entangled in a network of "Imposture," "Mistake," "Forgery," and "Uncertainty" (4–5). In this passage, this ongoing undercutting of authority is labeled as an inevitable "Lye": "I cannot but own 'tis just, that if I tell a Story in Print for a Truth which proves otherwise, unless I, at the same time, give proper Caution to the Reader, by owning the Uncertainty of my Knowledge in the matter of fact, 'tis I impose upon the World: my Relator is innocent, and the Lye is my own" (4–5). This intersection—or even

---

2. Daniel Defoe, *The Storm*, ed. Richard Hamblyn (London: Penguin Books, 2005), 3. Subsequent references to this source are cited parenthetically in the text.

crossfire—of human authority and unpredictable other-than-human uncertainty is the distinctive hallmark of both of these imaginary encounters with the weather.

I

But the weather is a distinctively human-centered discursive topic for the human imagination. Well beyond and long predating "A City Shower" and *The Storm*, the representation of the weather has been used as a tool to shape, manage, and understand human being, consistently invoking a premise of human priority.[3] From the classical period onward, and even to the present day, accounts of climate have focused on the equation of human ailments or character traits with climatic events.[4] For Swift,

> A coming Show'r your shooting Corns presage,
> Old Aches throb, your hollow Tooth will rage. (ll. 9–10)

This association of human "Aches" with changes in the weather is a longstanding trope. For Joseph Addison in *Spectator* 440 (1712), for example, "another of the Company . . . knew by a Pain in his Shoulder that we should have some Rain."[5] And human character traits are also conventionally attributed to climate. Addison attributes the human trait of jealousy to the tropics in *Spectator* 170 (1711):

> Jealousy is no Northern Passion, but rages most in those Nations that lie nearest to the Influence of the Sun. . . . Between the Tropicks . . . lie the hottest Regions of jealousy, which as you come Northward cools all along with the Climate, till you scarce meet with any thing like it in the Polar Circle. Our own Nation is very temperately situated in this Respect, and if we meet with

---

3. On climatic determinism, see Mark Harrison, *Climates and Constitutions: Health, Race, Environment and British Imperialism in India, 1600–1850* (Oxford: Oxford University Press, 2003).

4. For a current comment on "climate determinism," see Simon Donner, "The Ugly History of Climate Determinism Is Still Evident Today," *Scientific American* 24 (June 2020), https://www.scientificamerican.com/article/the-ugly-history-of-climate-determinism-is-still-evident-today/.

5. Joseph Addison, *Spectator* 440 (July 25, 1712), in *The Spectator*, vol. 4, ed. Donald F. Bond (Oxford, UK: Clarendon, 1965), 47.

some few disordered with the Violence of this Passion, they are not the proper Growth of our Country.[6]

And more systematically in *Remarks on the Influence of Climate . . . [on] Mankind* (1781), the physician William Falconer offers an exhaustive treatise on the role of climate in shaping—according to his table of contents—human disposition, manners, morals, intellectual faculties, laws, government, and religion. In the chapter on the "general state of morals in different climates," for instance, Falconer lays out the generally "agreed" assumption:

> In point of morality in general, it is . . . agreed, that the manners of cold climates far exceed those of warm; in the latter, the passions are naturally very strong, and likewise kept in a perpetual state of irritation from the high degree of sensibility that prevails, which causes a great multiplication of crimes, by multiplying the objects of temptation. . . . In cold climates the desires are but few, in comparison, and not often a very immoral kind; and those repressed with less difficulty, as they are seldom very violent. In temperate climates, the passions are in a middle state, and generally inconstant in their nature; sufficiently strong, however, to furnish motives for action, though not so powerful as to admit of no restraint from considerations of prudence, justice, or religion.[7]

David Hume in "Of National Characters" (1753) cites the pervasiveness of this "suppos'd" shaping effect of climate on human character while ultimately seeking to discredit it: "By *physical* causes I mean those qualities of the air and climate, which are suppos'd to work insensibly on the temper, by altering the tone and habit of the body, and giving a particular complexion, which tho' reflection and reason may sometimes overcome, will yet prevail among the generality of mankind, and have an influence on their manners."[8] The effect of these assumptions about the connection of weather with human character is to frame the representation of the environment around the

---

6. Joseph Addison, *Spectator* 170 (September 14, 1711), in *The Spectator*, vol. 2, ed. Donald F. Bond (Oxford, UK: Clarendon, 1965), 172.

7. William Falconer, *Remarks on the Influence of Climate . . . [on] Mankind* (London: C. Dilly, 1781), 25–26.

8. David Hume, "Essay XXIV: Of National Characters," in *Essays and Treatises on Several Subjects*, vol. 1 (London: A. Millar, 1753), 278. See John G. Hayman, "Notions on National Characters in the Eighteenth Century Author(s)," *Huntington Library Quarterly* 35 (1971): 13.

human, often limiting the depiction of weather in the text to a simple equation with a human condition.

Meanwhile, other aspects of eighteenth-century literary history highlight the depiction of the environment in poetic form. The representation of "nature" is subject to significant change in the course of this period, as the aesthetic intensity of the romantic movement generates an association between the realm of the environment and the distinctive genius of the poet. Literary representations of storms dramatize this shift. In a survey of poetical storms, Christopher Thacker documents the "revolution in attitudes [in the course of the eighteenth century] which had until then been virtually unchanged since the beginnings of literature." As Thacker demonstrates, storms before the eighteenth century typically offer an aesthetic experience that "repels the observer in every way." But with the rise of the romantic movement, "the absolute of rejection has changed to an enthusiasm every bit as absolute": "whereas, at the time of Bishop Burnet, the storm was evidence of evil, of man's sin and the Creator's anger, by the time of the romantics it was the opposite, the crowning evidence of the sublimity of nature and a symbol of man's most rarefied poetic aspiration. It had become that part of nature with which the poet would most eagerly be united, and into which he would have himself dissolved."[9]

In keeping with this eagerness, James Thomson's widely read georgic poem *The Seasons* (1726–30) supplies a transitional illustration. The second two couplets of the first edition of "Winter" explicitly "welcome" these literary storms:

> *Vapours*, and *Clouds*, and *Storms*: Be these my theme,
> These, that exalt the Soul to solemn Thought,
> And heavenly musing. Welcome kindred Glooms!
> Wish'd, wint'ry, Horrors, hail![10]

But *The Seasons* also depicts the storm in terms of human loss, destruction, and death. In a crucial scene from "Autumn," the "potent blast . . . further swells, / and in one mighty stream, invisible / . . . Impetuous rushes o'er the

---

9. Christopher Thacker, "'Wish'd, Wint'ry, Horrors': The Storm in the Eighteenth Century," *Comparative Literature* 19 (1967): 36, 56–57.

10. James Thomson, "Winter: Text of the First Edition," in *The Complete Poetical Works of James Thomson*, ed. J. Logie Robertson (Oxford: Oxford University Press, 1908), 228, ll. 3–6; cited also in Thacker, "Wish'd, Wint'ry, Horrors," 39.

sounding world." This storm—using the same tropes of enumeration and of confluence that we will identify in Defoe's *Storm* and Swift's "City Shower"—takes innumerable "herds" and "harvests" down a "rushing tide":

> Still over head
> The mingling tempest weaves its gloom, and still
> The deluge deepens; till the fields around
> Lie sunk and flatted in the sordid wave.
> Sudden the ditches swell; the meadows swim.
> Red from the hills innumerable streams
> Tumultuous roar, and high above its banks
> The river lift—before whose rushing tide
> Herds, flocks, and harvests, cottages and swains
> Roll mingled down.[11]

The Seasons looks toward the enthusiastic merger of poet and tempest of the romantic movement but participates also in the powerful tropes connecting the storm with the depiction of human disaster.[12]

Storms reflect an ongoing opportunity for the representation of human authority over or intensity toward or explanation of "nature." This chapter seeks to steer the storm past these dimensions of the human cultural imaginary. The two literary storms examined here—the "City Shower" and *The Storm*—as we shall see, exceed such a framing, replacing these limitations on the representation of the environmental realm and these assertions of human authority over or appropriation of that representation with confusion, impossibility, excess, and even moments of other-than-human force or vitality or "voice."

II

When Swift's "Description of a City Shower" was first published in Richard Steele's *Tatler* on October 17, 1710, it was introduced in the context of the

---

11. James Thomson, "Autumn," in *Complete Poetical Works*, 145, ll. 332–41.

12. Tobias Menely understands Thomson's representation of destruction as his recognition of a "disequilibrium in nature that could not be fully incorporated within the harmonious universe of Newtonian physicotheology or confident proclamations of national progress." See Menely, *Climate and the Making of Worlds: Toward a Geohistorical Poetics* (Chicago: University of Chicago Press, 2021), 121.

great storms of Virgil's *Georgics* and *Aeneid*.[13] Swift's poem clearly evokes the venerable scenario of the *Aeneid*'s momentous storm, which in that poem leads directly to the consummation of Aeneas and Dido's love. Here is Dryden's translation:

> Mean time, the gath'ring Clouds obscure the Skies;
> From Pole to Pole the forky Lightning flies;
> The ratling Thunders rowl; and *Juno* pours
> A wintry Deluge down; and sounding Show'rs.
> . . . .
> The rapid Rains, descending from the Hills,
> To rolling Torrents raise the creeping Rills.
> The Queen and Prince, as Love or Fortune guides,
> One common Cavern in her Bosom hides.[14]

Swift's poem recollects this passage, echoing the "torrents" as well as the "rattling" or "clattering" sound effects of Virgil/Dryden's storm and then directly evokes the *Aeneid*'s trademark account of the Trojan horse:

> Box'd in a Chair the Beau impatient sits,
> While Spouts run clatt'ring o'er the Roof by Fits;
> And ever and anon with frightful Din
> The Leather sounds, he trembles from within.
> So when *Troy* Chair-men bore the Wooden Steed,
> Pregnant with *Greeks*, impatient to be freed,
> . . . .
> *Laoco'n* struck the Outside with his Spear,
> And each imprison'd Hero quak'd for Fear. (ll. 43–52)

"A City Shower" thus brings the classical storm to present-day London, replacing the heroic Virgilian protagonists with damp contemporary Londoners,

---

13. Describing accounts of storms and showers, Steele cites Virgil: *"Virgil's Land Shower* is likewise the best in its Kind. It is indeed a Shower of Consequence, and contributes to the main Design of the Poem, but cutting off a tedious Ceremonial, and bringing Matters to a speedy Conclusion between Two Potentates of different Sexes." Richard Steele, *Tatler* 238 (October 17, 1710), in *The Tatler*, vol. 3, ed. Donald F. Bond (Oxford, UK: Clarendon, 1987), 225.

14. John Dryden, *Aeneid* 4.231–40, in *The Works of John Dryden*, vol. 5, *Poems: The Works of Virgil in English*, ed. William Frost, textual ed. Vinton A. Dearing (Berkeley: University of California Press, 1987), 259–60.

using this ironic juxtaposition with the classical original—in the same destabilizing manner as the "pensive cat"—to undermine the assertion of orderly confidence and control in the representation of climate.[15]

In contrast to the lyric form of "A City Shower," *The Storm* is one of the period's most extended narrative engagements with a specific environmental experience. As Defoe's first sustained narrative work, *The Storm* establishes some of the fundamental aspects of the innovative representation of temporality and immediacy distinctive of Defoe's subsequent novels.[16] *The Storm* arrived in literary history as an almost direct effect of what meteorological history now understands to have been an extratropical cyclone, which moved across England and Wales in the hours between midnight and six o'clock in the morning on November 26 and 27, 1703. The force of the wind, which reached 110 miles per hour, resulted in extensive losses of structures on land and vessels on the sea and caused the deaths of more than eight thousand human beings and many more thousands of other-than-human beings—fish, birds, livestock, and other animals.[17]

Immediately and directly, Defoe took up the human experience of this event through his developing expertise as a journalist. Within a week of the storm, he had placed notices in the *Daily Courant* and the *London Gazette* requesting of

all Gentlemen of the Clergy, or others, who have made any observations of this Calamity, that they would transmit as distinct an Account as possible, of what they have observed. . . . All Gentlemen that are pleas'd to send any such Accounts, are desired to write no Particulars but that they are well satisfied to be true, and to set their Names to the Observations they send, which the Undertakers of this Work [an exact and faithful Collection] promise shall be faithfully Recorded.[18]

---

15. On the poem's references to Virgil and Milton, see John I. Fischer, "Apparent Contraries: A Reading of Swift's 'A Description of a City Shower,'" *Tennessee Studies in Literature* 19 (1974): 21–34.

16. See Aino Makikalli, "Between Non-fiction and Fiction: Experiences of Temporality in Defoe's Writings on the Great Storm of 1703," in *Positioning Defoe's Non-fiction: Form, Function, Genre*, ed. Makikalli and Andreas K. E. Mueller (Newcastle upon Tyne, UK: Cambridge Scholars, 2011), 107–22; and Paula Backscheider, *Daniel Defoe: Ambition and Innovation* (Lexington: University Press of Kentucky, 1986), 86–87.

17. See Richard Hamblyn, introduction to Defoe, *Storm*, x–xii; Hubert Lamb and Knud Frydendahl, *Historic Storms of the North Sea, British Isles and Northwest Europe* (Cambridge: Cambridge University Press, 1991), 59–72; and Martin Brayne, *The Greatest Storm* (Phoenix Mill, UK: Sutton, 2002).

18. *Daily Courant* 409 (December 2, 1703); *London Gazette* 3972 (December 2–6, 1703); cited in Hamblyn, introduction to Defoe, *Storm*, xxiii.

Defoe received around sixty eyewitness accounts, and he edited, rewrote, and quoted these to produce *The Storm*. Richard Hamblyn in his introduction to the Penguin edition posits that there is at some points a "high level of fabrication" even within the quoted materials; *The Storm* is a pioneering work of modern journalism, both in the promotion of reportage itself and in its manipulation.[19]

In *The Storm*'s engagement with the experience of this climatic event, it instantiates the immediate and pragmatic attention to the weather that arises as a facet of the development of the empirical practices associated with the new science. Robert Markeley outlines this range of practices for the study of the weather, especially relevant to members of the Royal Society but also practiced by ordinary citizens in proto-Enlightenment London. These included the recording and publishing of weather diaries, barometric and rainfall records, lists of death tolls resulting from inclement weather, bills for property damage, accounts of chemical reactions in the atmosphere, theories of "Subterraneall Storms," and, in general, the growing usage "in the eighteenth century [of] tables, graphs, and charts to buttress . . . discursive descriptions of the natural world."[20] Collectively, these discursive and empirical accounts initiate and then constitute the new modern science of weather—or meteorology—promoted and theorized by the Royal Society.[21]

In *The Storm*'s first long section, titled "The Storm," the narrative reproduces a set of secondhand summaries, including accounts of the "Originals of Winds," of the "Opinion of the ancients" regarding storms in Britain, and of the "Extent of this Storm, and from what Parts it was suppos'd to come; with some Circumstances as to the Time of it." But even in this historical and contextual section, chapter 3—"Of the Storm in General"—which

---

19. Hamblyn, introduction to Defoe, *Storm*, xxvii.

20. Robert Markeley, "'Casualties and Disasters': Defoe and the Interpretation of Climatic Instability," *Journal for Early Modern Cultural Studies* 8 (2008): 114. Markeley cites Frans De Bruyn, "The Classical Silva and the Generic Development of Scientific Writing in Seventeenth-Century England," *New Literary History* 32 (2001): 347–73; and De Bruyn, "From Georgic Poetry to Statistics and Graphs: Eighteenth-Century Representations and the 'State' of British Society," *Yale Journal of Criticism* 17 (2004): 107–39. On "Subterraneall Storms," Markeley quotes Ralph Bohun, *A Discourse Concerning the Origine and Properties of Wind* (1671).

21. See also Jan Golinski, "Time, Talk, and the Weather in Eighteenth-Century Britain," in *Weather, Climate, Culture* (Oxford, UK: Berg, 2003), 21.

occupies the center portion of this section, despite its impersonal title, is structured around an ongoing direct and personal account of the narrator's particular experiences in London on the night of the storm:

> The Collector of these Sheets narrowly escap'd the Mischief of a Part of the House, which fell on the Evening of that Day by the Violence of the Wind.... The author of this Relation was in a well-built brick House in the skirts of the City; and a Stack of Chimneys falling in upon the next Houses gave the House such a Shock, that they thought it was just coming down upon their Heads: but opening the Door to attempt an Escape into a Garden, the Danger was so apparent, that they all thought fit to surren-der to the Disposal of Almighty Providence, and expect their Graves in the Ruins of the House, rather than to meet most certain Destruction in the Open Garden . . . for the force of the Wind blew the Tiles point-blank.... The Author of this has seen Tiles blown from a House above thirty or forty Yards, and stuck from five to eight Inches into the solid Earth. (26, 30–31)

The second long section of *The Storm*, "Of the Effects of the Storm," is largely made up of the reported accounts that Defoe had gathered, subtitled accord-ing to locations, sorts of "Damages," and varieties of "remarkable Deliver-ances." But even here, again, Defoe inserts his own direct experience alongside these reports by other eyewitnesses. His personal account takes up the re-sponsibility and authority of the direct observer:

> The Author of this Collection had the curiosity the next day to view the place [the "Reaches of the River" where the "Wind had driven" the ships into one another "and laid them so upon one another as it were in heaps"] and to observe the posture they lay in, which nevertheless 'tis impossible to describe; there lay, by the best Account he could take, few less than 700 sail of Ships, some very great ones between *Shadwel* and *Limehouse* inclusive, the posture is not to be imagined, but by them that saw it. (137)

The result of this sort of insertion is a dispersed, repetitious mingling of modes of discourse, variously evoking an encyclopedic representation of an environmental event layered across raw and edited eyewitness reportage, first-hand accounts, historical summary, proto-meteorology, and data.

III

But in *The Storm*, even in the context of historical, personal, journalistic, or proto-meteorological discourse, the attempt to represent the experience of the environmental event constantly veers toward the indescribable. As we have seen in the narrator's account of the seven hundred ships wrecked in the river, despite this immediate and direct context, the sight is "nevertheless . . . impossible to describe." This impossibility is introduced at the very outset of the narrative, in the preface, when the speaker offers a "confession": "I confess here is room for abundance of Romance. . . . . When Nature was put into so much Confusion, and the Surface of the Earth and Sea felt such extraordinary a Disorder, innumerable Accidents would fall out that till the like Occasion happen may never more be seen, and unless a like Occasion had happen'd could never before been heard of" (6).

This premise of impossibility is ubiquitous in this text. In the chapter titled "Of the Storm in General," which we have already seen—despite its title—to follow the speaker's personal experiences on the night of the storm, human expression is explicitly conceded to be impossible: "In short, Horror and Confusion seiz'd upon all, whether on Shore or at Sea: No Pen can describe it, no Tongue can express it" (53). And the narrator highlights this concession to impossibility even after the witnesses' immediate "Fears were . . . abated":

> About Eight a Clock in the Morning it ceased so much, that our Fears were also abated, and People began to peep out of Doors; but 'tis impossible to express the Concern that appear'd in every Place. . . . The next Day or Two was almost entirely spent in the Curiosity of the People, in viewing the Havock the Storm had made, which was so universal in *London*, and especially in the Out-Parts, that nothing can be said sufficient to describe it. (34)

Later, in the second section, "The Effects of the Storm," at the end of the compilation of letters titled "Of the Damages to the City of London, and parts adjacent," the narrator-journalist admits that, even after the exhaustive reportage that he has presented, "It has been impossible to give an exact relation." And he goes on here to repeat, "'Tis impossible to describe the general Calamity, and the most we can do is, to lead our Reader to supply by his

Immagination what we omit" (105–9). If the journalist-narrator—and all the "People" of London—cannot describe the scene of the storm, this suggestion that the reader's "Immagination" might reach that end is, almost explicitly, unconvincing. But this "Calamity"—inaccessible to the human imagination—emerges from *The Storm* in the "omissions" of the counterhuman imaginary.

The most conventional rationale for this evocation of impossibility is in the doctrinal citation of divine power—the explicit disavowal of human understanding in favor of the invisible rationale of God. In the narrator's account of the "causes and original of winds," for instance, he concedes human authority to another "Author": "Nature plainly refers us beyond her Self, to the Mighty Hand of Infinite Power, the Author of Nature, and Original of all Causes" (11). And indeed, the citation of divine power in relation to environmental or geologic events is a conventional recourse in this period. In Markeley's analysis of the representation of climatic instability in *The Storm*, he describes the ways in which divine inscrutability became compatible with empirical investigation and scientific speculation. For voluntarist theology, the "casualties and disasters" of the storm both prove divine omnipotence and at the same time inspire the study of the natural world as a means of appreciating those operations of the divine will.[22] Even in Newton's view, as Markeley elsewhere shows, "God's interventions both revealed the mysterious workings of grace and directed the practitioners of 'physico-theology' to study the natural world in order to understand, as far as possible, the second causes through which the divine will operated."[23] For *The Storm*, however, the "study" that would bring the experience of this climatic event within human understanding and authority is a distant and unrealized prospect whose evocation only highlights this narrative's contrapuntal scenario of impossibility.

In fact, that repeated phrase—"impossible to describe"—could be seen as the term of art for the representation of storms and environmental events in this period of literary history. *The Storm* exemplifies this impossibility with a special discursive pervasiveness: "impossible to describe" constitutes a coun-

---

22. Markeley, "Casualties and Disasters," 108. Courtney Weiss Smith provides a detailed account of role of God's will in Anne Finch's poem on the great storm of 1703. See Smith, "Anne Finch's Descriptive Turn," *The Eighteenth Century* 57 (2016): 251–65, esp. 254–55.

23. Markeley, "Casualties and Disasters," 104. See also Markeley, *Fallen Languages: Crises of Representation in Newtonian England, 1660–1740* (Ithaca, NY: Cornell University Press, 1993), 178–256.

terexplanatory scenario that extends across this complex work's whole range
of discourses and modes of representation.

IV

The accompaniment to "impossible to describe" is the contrapuntal theme
of counterhuman interrelationality—processes of assemblage that juxtapose,
entangle, combine, and replicate other-than-human objects, beings, events,
fluids, vapors, and "filths." "A City Shower" ultimately labels the cumulative
experience of this interrelationality as a "huge Confluent" or, ultimately and
more graphically, as a "Torrent" or a "tumbling":

> They [Filths of all Hues and Odours], as each Torrent drives,
>   with rapid Force,
> From *Smithfield*, or St. *Pulchre*'s shape their Course,
> And in huge Confluent joined at *Snow-Hill* Ridge,
> Fall from the *Conduit* prone to *Holborn-Bridge*.
> Sweepings from Butchers Stalls, Dung, Guts, and Blood,
> Drown'd Puppies, stinking Sprats, all drench'd in Mud,
> Dead Cats, and Turnip-Tops come tumbling down the Flood. (ll. 57–63)

The random assemblage of the poem's last couplet—dung, guts, blood, pup-
pies, fish, cats, turnips—entangles without connecting and proposes a relationality that cannot be defined. In fact, first, before the "tumbling" or
interrelational turbulence of this passage, human beings themselves are
impelled into a random relationality by the storm. Various human beings—
the "daggled Females," the "Templar spruce," and the "tuck'd-up Semp-
stress," as well as the "triumphant Tories and desponding Whigs"—cross
paths and share space and "commence Acquaintance" (ll. 35–42). And even
before human beings join this "torrent," the indistinguishable components
of the geo-environmental realm—"Dust and Rain"—find their own unconventional interrelation on the poet's coat:

> Not yet, the Dust had shun'd th' unequal Strife,
> But, aided by the Wind, fought still for Life;
> And wafted with its Foe by violent Gust,
> 'Twas doubtful which was Rain, and which was Dust. (ll. 23–26)

In *The Storm*, the same counterhuman interrelationality—among water, fish, birds, trees, and human beings—accompanies the same "huge Confluent." In chapter 4, "Of the Extent of this Storm,"

> The Water in the River of *Thames*, and other Places, was in a very strange manner blown up into the Air: Yea, in the new Pond in *James's Park*, the Fish to the Number of at least two Hundred, were blown out and lay by the Bankside, whereof many were Eye-witnesses.
>
> At *Moreclack* in *Surry*, the *Birds*, as they attempted to fly, were beaten down to the Ground by the Violence of the Wind.
>
> At *Epping* in the County of *Essex*, a very great Oak was blown down, which of it self was raised again, and doth grow firmly at this Day.
>
> At *Taunton*, a great Tree was blown down, the upper Part wherof rested upon a Brick or Stone-wall, and after a little time, by the force of the Wind, the lower part of the Tree was blown quite over the Wall.
>
> In the City of *Hereford*, several persons were, by the Violence of the Wind, borne up from the Ground; one Man (as it is credibly reported) at least six Yards. (46)

This ongoing juxtaposition of oak tree and other-than-human and human beings projects the same indistinguishability as the "Confluent" of "A City Shower"—one item after another or all items together in a descriptive "torrent"—in a scenario beyond or irrelevant to human agency or to the human authority of the narrator-journalist to propose a hierarchic or anthropocentric pattern. As we shall see, this passage, like the final couplet of "A City Shower," could stand in for the discursive experience of *The Storm* as a whole—its ongoing repetitions, enumerations, lists, and series of events, locations, objects, and beings.

The multiplicity and turbulence that emerge in both of these representations of undefined, other-than-human "force" are a distinctive effect that is illuminated by recent perspectives on discontinuity in modern scientific and philosophic thought, as we have seen in our earlier analysis of the counterhuman impossibility that emerges in Alexander Pope's *The Dunciad* and in the poetry of the Lisbon earthquake. Michel Serres in his account of "the birth of physics" describes the persistence of notions of "discontinuity, multiplicity and contingency" from ancient atomism to modern quantum physics and helps us understand how human representation might exceed linearity and include an uncertainty that goes beyond the human. According to David Webb and William Ross's summary of Serres's argument, "The world to which [ancient atomism and modern physics] bears witness . . . is a place of turbulent flows, of chaos. . . . There is . . . no unilinear development and therefore no single frame of reference within which all events may be encompassed. There cannot even be a reliable rule of translation by which one can navigate from one frame or region to another, or between the local and the global."[24]

The Storm generates a version of this anti-encompassing counterhuman world in its representation of the "huge confluents" of varied, dispersed, undistinguished items like the list of fish, birds, trees, and persons that we observed earlier. But beyond the dispersed list, the narrative also offers lists of lists—that is, lists of separate lists, each of which represents a group of items or structures or architectural features connected by common features or a common agent of destruction: on the land (windows, stonework, doors, steeples, pews, church spires, pulpits, roof tiles; 43–33); on the water ("Ships of all sorts," colliers, coasters, store ships, transports, tenders, men of war, "*East India* Men," and merchant men; 51–52); in the countryside (barns, fruit trees, oaks, ash, ricks of corn). The list of barns, for example, includes this enumeration:

> From *Tewksbury* it is certified, that an incredible Number of Barns have been blown down in the small Towns and Villages thereabouts. At *Twyning*, at least eleven Barns are blown down. In *Ashchurch* Parish seven or eight. At *Lee*, five. At *Norton*, a very great Number, three whereof belonging to one Man. The great Abby-Barn also at *Tewksbury* is blown down.
>
> It is credibly reported, that within a very few Miles Circumference in *Worcestershire*, about an hundred and forty Barns are blown down. At *Finchinfield* in *Essex*, which is but an ordinary Village, about sixteen Barns were blown down. Also in a Town called *Wilchamsted* in the County of *Bedford* (a very small Village) fifteen Barns at least are blown down. But especially the Parsonage Barns went to wrack in many Places throughout the Land: In a few Miles Compass in *Bedfordshire*, and so in *Northamptonshire*, and other Places, eight, ten, and twelve are blown down; and at *Yielding Parsonage* in

24. David Webb and William Ross, introduction to *The Birth of Physics*, by Michel Serres, trans. Webb and Ross (Lanham, MD: Rowman and Littlefield, 2018), 3–7 (originally published 1977).

the County of *Bedford* (out of which was thrust by Oppression and Violence the late Incumbent) all the Barns belonging to it are down. The instances also of this kind are innumerable, which we shall therefore forbear to make further mention of. (44–45)

"Innumerable" in these lists is the equivalent of "impossible to describe," placing this set of items in a realm beyond the human imagination and explicitly precluding "further mention" of these barns, which thereby and at that point enter the counterhuman realm of impossibility.

These lists level humans with all the other lists of items—barns, ships, church steeples, sheep, and forests. Here is the list of human deaths, according to the "Article"—or common agent—of falling roofs or chimneys:

Under the Disaster of this Article [falling stacks of Chimneys], it seems most proper to place the Loss of the Peoples Lives, who fell in this Calamity. . . .

One Woman was kill'd by the Fall of a Chimney in or near the palace of St. *James's*. . . .

Nine Souldiers were hurt, with the Fall of the Roof of the Guard-house at *Whitehall*, but none of them died.

A Distiller in *Duke-Street*, with his Wife, and Maid-servant, were all buried in the Rubbish of a Stack of Chimneys, which forced all the Floors, and broke down to the Bottom of the House. . . .

One Mr. *Dyer*, a Plaisterer in *Fetter-Lane*, finding the Danger he was in by the shaking of the House, jumpt out of Bed to save himself; and had, in all Probability, Time enough to have got out of the House, but staying to strike a Light, a Stack of Chimneys fell in upon him, kill'd him, and wounded his Wife.

Two Boys at one Mr. *Purefoy's*, in *Cross-Street Hutton-Garden*, were both kill'd, and buried in the Rubbish of a Stack of Chimneys; and a third very much wounded.

A Woman in *Jewin-Street*, and Two Persons more near *Aldersgate-Street*, were kill'd; the first, as it is reported, by venturing to run out of the House into the Street; and the other Two by the Fall of a House.

In *Threadneedle-Street*, one Mr. *Simpson*, a Scrivener, being in Bed and fast a-sleep, heard nothing of the Storm; but the rest of the Family being more sensible of Danger, some of them went up, and wak'd him. . . . But he too fatally sleepy, and consequently unconcern'd at the Danger, told them, he did not apprehend any Thing; and so . . . could not be prevailed with to rise: they had not been gone many Minutes out of his Chamber, before the Chimneys fell in, broke through the Roof over him, and kill'd him in his Bed.

A Carpenter in *White-Cross-Street* was kill'd almost in the same Manner, by a Stack of Chimneys of the *Swan* Tavern, which fell into his House; it was reported, That his Wife earnestly desir'd him not to go to Bed; . . . but then finding himself very heavy, he would go to Bed against all his Wife's Intreaties; after which . . . [he] was kill'd in his Bed: and his Wife, who would not go to Bed, escap'd. (58–59)

These lists of course fail actually to describe the unrepresentable agency of the storm: the environmental realm is a projection from exhaustive recitations of innumerability and dispersal. Examining Anne Finch's poem on the same storm of 1703—"Upon the Hurricane" (1713)—Courtney Weiss Smith also describes an extended scenario of dispersal and multiplicity, arguing that Finch represents "the storm as a complex constellation that draws together not only winds, God, and human actions, but a whole range of other relevant agents and forces: the Bible, the past, Kidder [Bishop of Bath who was killed in the storm], oaths of allegiance, chimney stacks, us, our sins, her guesses, death, fallen branches, vapors, and local motion."[25] The "gathering" that Smith describes in "Upon the Hurricane" engages an "active, material" force.[26] Like the lists and the turbulences that we have observed in *The Storm* and the "City Shower," they project a vitality, but it is a counterhuman vitality that exceeds or eludes human representation and that goes beyond the notion that the poem discovers or promotes a human-centered "richer understanding of the world," which Smith concludes from Finch's work.[27]

V

Innumerability and *impossibility* pervade "A City Shower" and *The Storm*, offering an imaginative experience beyond encompassing order and apart from narrative authority. And in both texts, this counterhuman experience of climate holds the announced subject—the "shower" or the "storm"—beyond

---

25. Smith, "Anne Finch's Descriptive Turn," 255.

26. "The poet does not project onto blank screens, so much as she 'gathers' together and attempts to at least partially understand the complexity that resides in God's creation—a creation that is in itself active, material, and moral" (Smith, 261).

27. Smith, 263.

or apart from human representation: the "shower" or the "storm" rarely makes an appearance that a reader might register as direct or concrete. And the few brief occasions in each text when the environmental event of the title is directly portrayed enhance the counterhuman impact of *impossibility* by emphasizing, by omission, how rarely or briefly or partially or incommensurately the "shower" or the "storm" is within human view, how consistently the environmental realm exceeds or eludes the human.

In "A City Shower," the "shower" itself is represented or characterized through a brief evocation of a "force." The passage that introduces the "huge Confluent" suggests the role of this "force":

> Now from all Parts the swelling Kennels flow,
> And bear their Trophies with them as they go:
> Filth of all Hues and Odours seem to tell
> What Streets they sail'd from, by the Sight and Smell.
> They, as each Torrent drives with rapid Force,
> From *Smithfield,* or *St. Pulchre*'s shape their course,
> And in huge Confluent joined at *Snow-Hill* Ridge,
> Fall from the *Conduit* prone to *Holborn-Bridge.* (ll. 53–60)

Specifically here, the "Torrent" that "drives" the "Trophies" from their dispersed locations throughout the London sewers to their point of assembly or "Confluent" at "*Snow-Hill* Ridge" operates by means of a "rapid Force"—an irresistible power that registers a momentum inherent in the storm and that seems to be at one with the agency of "torrent." This force is both dispersed and vital, resembling the force "inertly strong" of the Mighty Mother Dulness in *The Dunciad* or the inherent power of matter in Newton's laws of motion, which we have observed in conjunction with the self-efficacy of matter in *Robinson Crusoe.* In "A City Shower," this "force" has some specific characteristics: it is "violent"—"wafted by its foe by violent gust" (25)—and it may be accompanied by certain dramatic sound effects that impinge upon the vulnerable or even captive human figures in the poem:

> Boxed in a chair the beau impatient sits,
> While spouts run clattering o'er the roof by fits,
> And ever and anon with frightful din
> The leather sounds; he trembles from within. (ll. 43–46)

We have noted the connection between this poem's "clattering" and the "rat-tling" in the *Aeneid*'s crucial storm. In addition, this "clattering" or "fright-ful din" briefly supplies the "city shower" with a "voice" of its own. The titular climatic entity of the poem, then, is heard but not seen, is violent with-out agency and vital without accord with or relation to human or living vitality.

The Storm gives the same, brief, auditory representation of its protagonist. In the chapter "Of the Storm in General," "Others thought they heard it thunder. 'Tis confess'd, the Wind by its unusual Violence made such a noise in the Air as had a resemblance to Thunder; and 'twas observ'd, the roaring had a Voice as much louder than usual, as the Fury of the Wind was greater than was ever known: the Noise had also something in it more formidable; it sounded aloft, and roar'd not very much unlike remote Thunder" (32). Or in the section "Of the Damages in the Country," "as to Thunder the Noise the Wind made, was so Terrible, and so Unusual, that I will not say, people might not mistake it for Thunder; but I have not met with any, who will be positive that they heard it Thunder" (109). Here the "Noise" of the storm evokes the same "unusual Violence" that is attributed to the storm of "A City Shower," again through an indeterminate agency, which in this passage is evoked through the use of the anthropomorphic term "Voice"—a corollary to the audible "clattering" of the storm in "A City Shower." The "Voice" of the wind in *The Storm* is so inherently problematic as to generate explicit con-fusion in the human observers and in the text itself: witnesses "thought they heard" this "Voice"; they cannot seem to agree on what they may have heard; and even the journalist-narrator cannot coherently express his reportage of this experience of the sound of the wind in straightforward, positive terms: "I will not say people might not mistake it. . . . I have not met with any, who will be positive." Both "A City Shower" and *The Storm* are pointing to a coun-terhuman "force" or "violence" or even perhaps a "Voice" that is mostly off-screen, distanced from and even repudiated by the human witnesses and the reporter, but indirectly endowed with an elusive autonomy and vitality.

As we have seen, these two works of human creativity cite human author-ity, reflect human awareness, engage ongoing human science and record keeping, and build on historical human discursive and literary traditions. They are powerful assertions of the cultural imaginary of their time as it turns to an engagement with the realm of climate. But they also agitate, undermine, and exceed these human claims, in ways that indicate how the environment escapes from, is separate from, cannot be accommodated to human authority or human representation and in ways that offer a view of a counterhuman imaginative experience, an experience of a vitality beyond the human.

Coda

Just Beyond

Across the texts that this study has explored, the relationship between human creativity and the possibility of an other-than-human vitality—between the cultural imaginary and the counterhuman imaginary—has taken a range of shapes. In the juxtaposition of the two accounts of storms—by Swift and Defoe—we observed an other-than-human realm extrapolated out of failures of human authority and human-centered coherence, as a vast unfocused confluent backdrop to the human perspective. Similarly, the poetry of the Lisbon earthquake of 1755 points toward a force inaccessible to human scenarios of order and coherence, through a persistent formal oxymoron that juxtaposes autonomous multiplicity with sudden, immediate, transformative power. *The Dunciad* offers a much more sustained, detailed, intense, ongoing experience of that power—represented as "uncreation" and displayed as an other-than-human "new world" emerging from the self-generative force of matter. *Robinson Crusoe* enacts a self-creative other-than-human vitality by setting matter in motion through the persistent repetition of irresistible succession. And both the lapdog lyric and the circulation narrative, in corollary ways, cross boundaries of being through a formal melding of the human and the other-than-human. The common result in each instance—the vast unfocused backdrop, the sustained "new world," the self-creative vitality, the melding of human and other-than-human—is the projection of a counterhuman realm just outside the region of human creative purpose, just beyond explicit acknowledgment, just out of the reach of the human cultural imaginary.

This realm of *just beyond* calls for a new understanding of symptomatic reading. The notion of the cultural imaginary as it is deployed here accepts a core premise of symptomatic reading: that—quoting again from Cornelius Castoriadis—the "central signifying-signified" of human authority is a reflection of "each historical period, its singular manner of living, of seeing and of conducting its own existence, its world, and its relations with this world."[1] The "real conditions of existence" that are obscured by that "central signifying-signified" are the aim of symptomatic reading, which entails, as Fredric Jameson has said, the "diagnostic revelation of terms or nodal points implicit in the ideological system which have . . . remained unrealized in the surface of the text, which have failed to become manifest in the logic of the narrative, and which we can therefore read as what the text represses."[2]

The concept of the cultural imaginary systematically enforces the framing of human assertions of authority and human claims to "indisputable and undisputed meaning." But the backdropping, the self-generative "new world," the boundary melding, and the material vitality that we have seen to characterize the forms of the counterhuman imaginary in this study are not fully compatible with those "unrealized" "nodal points"—with the "real conditions of [human] existence" or even of human history—that are central to the methodology of symptomatic reading. Two recent positions on the relevance of symptomatic reading to the explication of this *just beyond* provide a triangulation of posthuman thinking around this particular theoretical challenge—the relation between the symptomatic and the counterhuman.

---

1. Cornelius Castoriadis, *The Imaginary Institution of Society*, trans. Karen Blamey (Cambridge, MA: MIT Press, 1987), 145 (originally published as *L'institution imaginaire de la société*, 1975).

2. Fredric Jameson, *Postmodernism; or The Cultural Logic of Late Capitalism* (Durham, NC: Duke University Press, 1991), 51, paraphrasing Louis Althusser, "Ideological State Apparatuses," in *Lenin and Philosophy* (New York: Monthly Review Press, 1972). Jameson, *The Political Unconscious: Narrative as a Socially Symbolic Act* (Ithaca, NY: Cornell University Press, 1981), 48.

In *Climate and the Making of Worlds*, Tobias Menely explicitly seeks to recover symptomatic reading for a "geohistorical poetics." Menely distinguishes his position from postcritique, which he exemplifies through citations of Sharon Marcus and Stephen Best's advocacy of "an interpretive practice concerned with textual surfaces" and their claim that "the critic must 'let go of the belief that texts and their readers have an unconscious,'" and of Rita Felski's rejection of "digging" for "what lies concealed."[3] Against these dismissals of symptomatic reading, Menely makes a strong and explicit claim that

> climate change requires a deepening, rather than a slackening, of symptomatic reading practices. . . . *Climate and the Making of Worlds* advances a mode of reading . . . concerned with the relation between the positivity of representation and the unconscious as an absence, break, or negation. Literary studies . . . is best able to contribute to the cross-disciplinary conversation organized around the climate crisis in its sensitivity to the limits of knowledge, the way silence and omission shadow saying, the exclusions that enable a representation of the world to be assembled, the conditions of synthesis but also nonresolution. To read critically, in light of the Anthropocene proposal, is to identify textual symptoms that express not historical but socioecological or even geohistorical contradiction.[4]

Silence, omission, exclusions, and nonresolution are for Menely some of the key characteristics of the expressions of "geohistorical contradiction"—the core conceptual scenario for his recovery of symptomatic reading.

Edna Duffy uses an account of Jameson's "political unconscious" to generate a similar recovery. She seeks to show, in "Modernism under Review: Fredric Jameson's *The Political Unconscious*," that Jameson's conceptualization of symptomatic reading accommodates "a modified Deleuzianism"—a potential engagement with "the imbrication of the human, the organic, and the planetary—the extensive network of life forms beyond the human in the environment and the interconnectedness of all living forms." This "more

---

3. Sharon Marcus and Stephen Best, "Surface Reading: An Introduction," *Representations* 108 (2009): 15; Rita Felski, *The Limits of Critique* (Chicago: University of Chicago Press, 2015), 5. See Tobias Menely, *Climate and the Making of Worlds: Toward a Geohistorical Poetics* (Chicago: University of Chicago Press, 2021), 18.

4. Menely, *Climate and the Making of Worlds*, 19–20.

flexible and Deleuzian Marxism" that Duffy claims for Jameson frames contradiction in relation to realms far beyond the human. Duffy's citation of Jameson's reading of Conrad exemplifies the new reach of contradiction: the unconscious realm of Conrad's *Nostromo* entails a reversal that reinforces "a new representational space."[5] Here, she uses Jameson's words:

> This reversal then draws ideology inside out like a glove, awakening an alien space beyond it, founding a new heaven and earth upon its inverted lining. In that stealthy struggle between ideology and representation, the ideological allegory of the ship as the civilized world on its way to doom is subverted by the unfamiliar sensorium which, like some new planet in the night sky, suggests senses and forms of libidinal gratification as unimaginable to us as the possession of additional senses, or the presence of non-earthly colors in the spectrum.[6]

This "alien space," this "new planet," and these "non-earthly colors"—like Menely's "silence," "omission," "exclusions," and "nonresolution"—point *just beyond* human vitality, human spaces, and human history. As Duffy concludes this extrapolation from Jameson, she extends her argument to make a larger claim for a "new concept of materiality" and a new proposal for a "cosmological criticism":

> This brings us . . . to the degree-zero of Jameson's new Marxist aesthetics. . . . Submerged beneath the surface of the argument here . . . is a new concept of materiality itself, struggling to be born. Invoking this "new heaven and new earth" implies a call for a cosmological criticism, in which new unimaginably vast spaces and extended times meet the history of the human senses in a dialectic of utopian desires and fears for the planet's future.[7]

Menely's "geohistorical contradiction" and Duffy's "cosmological criticism" both suggest a revised methodological attention to omission and to the "alien," and both offer an approach—via the geo-environmental realm—to the methodological challenge of *just beyond.*

---

5. Edna Duffy, "Modernism under Review: Fredric Jameson's *The Political Unconscious: Narrative as a Socially Symbolic Act* (1981)," *Modernist Cultures* 11 (2016): 145, 149, 158.

6. Jameson, *Political Unconscious*, 231; also cited in Duffy, "Modernism under Review," 158.

7. Duffy, "Modernism under Review," 159.

In reading beyond the "alien" and even beyond the cosmological to wider forms of the unimaginable—to the effects of uncreation, impossibility, and the self-efficacy of the other-than-human, the counterhuman imaginary sees the scope projected by "geohistorical contradiction" and "cosmological criticism" and seeks to give it a theory and a method. That that method itself lives *just beyond* any system that human theory can confirm might in turn be taken as its own confirmation.

INDEX

Page numbers followed by letter *f* refer to figures.

geohistorical poetics, 133
geologic events/forces: and counterhuman
  imaginary, 16, 18; and Pope's *Dunciad,*
  79–80; representation in literature, 3–4,
  20; self-organizing efficacy of, 16; and
  Voltaire's *Candide,* 100, 101. *See also*
  earthquake(s)
Gildon, Charles, 28–29
Golden Spy, The (Gildon), 28–29
gravitation/gravitational force: circulation
  narrative and engagement with, 28–29;
  Newton's conceptualization of, 19, 28, 49,
  55, 56–59; Pope's *Dunciad* and engagement
  with, 20, 75–77, 79, 80, 85, 88
great storm of 1703, 18; and advances in
  meteorology, 98, 119. *See also Storm, The*
  (Defoe)
Grusin, Richard, 6

Hamblyn, Richard, 119
Hartley, David, 59
Heidegger, Martin, notion of *das Krug,* 53–54,
  55, 63, 65
Hewitt, John, "Upon Cælia's having a little
  Dog in her Lap," 42
*History and Adventures of a Lady's Slippers and
  Shoes, The,* 32
*History and description of the most remarkable
  events relative to the earthquake that shook a
  great part of the earth at the end of the year
  1755* (Kant), 98
*History of Pompey the Little, or the Life and
  Adventures of a Lapdog, The* (Coventry), 34,
  35–37; and link to lapdog lyric, 38–39
Homer, Pope's *Dunciad* and, 71
Hultquist, Aleksondra, 10n17
human creativity: counterhuman imaginary
  embedded in, 12–13, 21; intrusion of
  other-than-human and, 21, 131–32;
  and vitality of matter, access to, 5–6,
  85–87
humanitarianism, rise of, 38
Hume, David: engagement with Defoe's
  Robinson Crusoe, 50; "Of National
  Characters," 114; in theological debate on
  powers of matter, 59
Hymns occasioned by the Earthquake (Wesley),
  91, 94, 95, 105–6
hyperhumanism, 15

ideology, Althusserian notion of, 8
individualist protagonist, primacy in
  eighteenth-century English literature, 18
innovation, literary: in circulation narrative
  and lapdog lyric, 38–39, 43–44; counterhuman imaginary and, 9–11, 17–21, 23, 24,
  27, 67, 131–32
interrelationality. *See* relationality/
  interrelationality
intimacy: counterhuman imaginary and
  reimagining of ideas about, 18–19, 44.
  See also cross-species intimacy
intuitive knowledge, thing-protagonist and,
  30, 32
Ionescu, Christina, 48
irony: in lapdog lyric, 39. *See also* satire
it-narratives, 23, 48. *See also* circulation
  narrative(s)

Jameson, Fredric, 5, 132, 133–34
jar/pot: in art, 46f; in Defoe's *Robinson
  Crusoe,* 52–53, 53n16, 63–64, 66; as form
  of knowledge and imagination, 68;
  Heidegger's conceptualization of, 53–54, 55,
  63, 65; as heuristic for modernity's theorization of materialism, 54–55; in poetry, 55n21
Johnstone, Charles, *Chrystal; or, The
  Adventures of a Guinea,* 29–32
journalism, modern, Defoe's *Storm* as
  pioneering work of, 118–19
just beyond, methodological challenge of,
  approaches to, 132–34

Kant, Immanuel, *History and description of
  the most remarkable events relative to the
  earthquake that shook a great part of the earth
  at the end of the year 1755,* 98
Keenleyside, Heather, 2–3, 85
Kett, Henry, "An Episode Taken from a
  Poem on the Earthquake at Lisbon," 96–97
Kinsley, William, 75
knowledge, intuitive, thing-protagonist and,
  30, 32
das Krug, Heidegger's conceptualization of,
  53–54, 55, 63, 65

labor theory of value, *Robinson Crusoe* and
  conceptualization of, 51
Lamb, Jonathan, *The Things Things Say,* 47–48

meteorology, great storm of 1703 and advances in, 98, 119

method/methodology: for analysis of counterhuman imaginary, Pope's *Dunciad* and, 20, 88–89; experimental, in Defoe's *Robinson Crusoe*, 63, 66; experimental, Newton's commitment to, 59–60, 66

Morgan, Thomas, 77

Motteux, Pierre, 77

movement/motion: as defining quality of things, 48; Newton's laws of, ambiguity in, 56. *See also* turbulence

multiplicity: and affect, new definition of, 43–44, 107; counterhuman and, 19, 20, 107, 109; in Defoe's *Storm*, 124; in earthquake poetry, 20, 102–4, 107, 124; in Finch's "Upon the Hurricane," 127; in Pope's *Dunciad*, 104, 107, 109; in Swift's "A City Shower," 123. *See also* assemblage(s); singularity, juxtaposed with multiplicity

nature: representation in literature, 3–5; romantic movement and representations of, 115–16. *See also* environmental events

new materialism, 1, 5–7, 16, 47–48; counterhuman imaginary and, 17; Defoe's iconic materialist vision and, 55; jar/pot in theorization of, 53–54; and new forms of political action and engagement, 86; Newtonian physics and, 67; Pope's *Dunciad* and, 87; quantum physics concepts and, 72; and reconceptualization of relationality, 72–73; *Robinson Crusoe*'s model and, 67; on transformative potential of actant thing, 25

Newton, Isaac: on agency/forces of matter, 19, 28–29, 56–59, 128; and circulation narrative, 28–29; and conception of matter, reshaping of, 49–50, 55–56, 75–76; and Defoe's *Robinson Crusoe*, 60; on divine omnipotence, 122; and experimental method, 59–60, 66; and Gildon's *The Golden Spy*, 28–29; and inherent powers of matter, debate about, 55; laws of motion, ambiguity in, 56; and new materialism, 67; and Pope's *Dunciad*, 75–77, 79, 80; study of alchemy, 57. *See also Optics*

Nonhuman Turn, The (Grusin), 6

Nostromo (Conrad), 134

novel, rise of, 18

objects. *See* thing(s)

"Of National Characters" (Hume), 114

omission, revised methodological attention to, 133, 134

"On a Lap-Dog" (Brown), 41

"On an Earthquake" (Clarke), 103, 106

"On the Death of a Lap-Dog" (Smedley), 40

ontological instability, lapdog lyric and, 39, 41–42

Optics (Newton), "Queries" to: on agency/forces of matter, 19, 28–29, 57; on experimental method, 59; as turning point in modern encounter with matter, 47, 49–50

other-than-human: affective convergence with human, in circulation narrative, 32–34; cultural imaginary and human representation of, 7–9, 14; disruptive forces within human cultural imaginary, 17–18; energy/force of, 19; and human creativity, 21, 131–32; meta-paradox in human claim to access, 5, 9, 12–13; ontological instability generated by, 39, 41–42; in Pope's *Dunciad*, 72; as protagonist, 23; representation in literature, 1–7, 17–21; unique literary access to, suggestions of, 6–7, 16. *See also* animal(s); matter; thing(s)

Other Things (Brown), 12

oxymoron, counterhuman, 92, 104–6, 107–9. *See also* singularity, juxtaposed with multiplicity

pet(s): as protagonist in circulation narrative, 34–37; rise in eighteenth century, 26. *See also* dog(s)

Philips, Edward, *The Adventures of a Black Coat*, 32

physics: counterhuman imaginary and, 67; as model for rejection of traditional subject/object rationales, 72; persistence of notions of discontinuity, multiplicity, and contingency in, 73–74, 124–25; relevance of ancient atomism to, 73–74. *See also* Newton, Isaac; quantum physics

Poem on the Earthquake at Lisbon (Biddulph), 92, 96, 102, 103–5

"Poem on the Late Earthquake at Lisbon, A," 94–95, 97, 103

"Poem on the Lisbon Disaster: *an Inquiry into the Maxim, 'Whatever is, is Right'*" (Voltaire), 99–100, 107–9; Rousseau's response to, 101–2